365 ways to live a simple and spiritual life

365 ways to live a simple and spiritual life

Madonna Gauding

 A GODSFIELD BOOK
www.godsfieldpress.com

I dedicate this book to my teacher Gehlek Rimpoche, to my mother, Virginia Gauding, and to Ann Wright, Brenda Rosen, Joanna Sandsmark, Aura Glaser and Stephen Nose.

First published in Great Britain in 2004 by Godsfield Press,
a division of Octopus Publishing Group Ltd
2–4 Heron Quays
Docklands
London E14 4JP

10 9 8 7 6 5 4 3 2 1

Printed and bound in China

ISBN 1 84181 242 0
EAN 9781841812427

Contents

Introduction **6**

365 ways to live a simpler and more spiritual life **10**

Sources **377**

Index **380**

Acknowledgements **384**

Introduction

This book is a record of my own journey towards a simpler and more spiritual life. And I feel that I have only just begun. In these pages you will find 365 ways to inspire you on your path. Obviously some will speak to you more than others, but I hope you will find all of them helpful in some way.

This guide covers a vast range of topics, from exploring your spirituality and your values to eating healthy and inexpensive food. You will find entries on debt reduction, preventive health care, over-consumption, addiction, healthy home environments, inexpensive entertainment and alternative gift-giving. You will find inspiration to help you define your own values and to nurture your heart and soul. I've found that, if you want to simplify your life and master the art of living, just about everything – from the profound to the practical – has to be on the table.

We live in the most complex culture in history, and we probably experience more activity and devour more information in one day than our ancestors did in a lifetime. And all this takes place in an intense electromagnetic haze of marketing, advertising and entertainment. We may have acquired a lot of 'stuff' and lead very stimulating lives, but real happiness and contentment are often eluding us. In fact, countless numbers of us are sleep-deprived, over-extended and deeply in debt; and stress-related diseases are rampant. Somewhere along the line we have confused standard of living with quality of life. And clearly they are not the same.

Like many of us, I woke up one day admitting that I wasn't really happy with my life. I felt stressed and overwhelmed; I had credit-card debt (which I am still paying off). I decided there must be a better way to live. My income is a modest one, and no one would consider me well off. I have prided myself on rejecting consumerism and being environmentally aware; I even shop in secondhand shops. Yet clearly I have listened to the incessant message to consume, with which the media bombards us on a daily basis. I too got the idea – from all the advertising around me – that I am entitled to a certain standard of living, even though I can't actually afford it. For instance, I *should* be able to buy a latté every day. Well, a latté each day adds up to a substantial amount over a year! And yes, I *should* be able to afford a 'cheap' lunch – add on another significant sum each year! It was my sense of entitlement to a certain middle-class lifestyle, as defined by someone else, combined with a belief that things outside me determine my happiness that got me into trouble.

The road to a balanced and spiritual life is different for each of us, and although dealing with money is central to the journey there is much more to creating real happiness. For once, we have to look inside and ask ourselves: What makes me truly happy? What qualities do I want to embody? How do I want to feel – emotionally, physically and spiritually – on a daily basis? What work would be most fulfilling,

regardless of the pay cheque? Are my possessions serving me or burdening me? How can I feel more connected to nature, to the people in my life and to my spiritual practice? What do I want to do before I die? What do I need to heal?

These questions may seem wildly unrelated to balancing your budget, but they are in fact deeply connected. When you find your answers, they will provide you with a blueprint for a life that's no longer driven by external pressures. You will have set your life on a course that is internally guided by your highest motives and deepest values, and which is uniquely and authentically yours.

How to use this book

In reading this book, follow your nose and see what speaks to you and what doesn't. If something grabs you, follow it up with further reading (see page 377), or research additional resources on the Web. Feel free to read this book from front to back, back to front, or simply to open a page every day to see what jumps out at you.

If possible, start a journal to keep track of the actions you take and any insights that you have about yourself or your lifestyle. List other resources that you find on your own. Every month assess what you've discovered or accomplished in the past 30 days. Keep track of improvements in your sense of well-being and overall happiness. Note any difficulties and resistance that you may be experiencing and try to explore the causes.

Lastly, find a support group. You may want to live a simpler, more spiritual life, but may find it difficult to swim against the swift current of social pressure. In other words, your friends and family may not understand what you're doing. We are all unique individuals, on our own journey, but we are also social animals — we need the support of others. Check on the Web for 'simplicity support groups' in your area.

You are, and always will be, a work in progress. Commit to simplifying your life and mastering the art of living, and you will begin an exciting, lifelong journey that will put you firmly in control of your own destiny. Take your time and, by all means, be kind to yourself. As my teacher Gehlek Rimpoche advises, 'Don't bite off more than you can chew.'

Good luck on your journey.

365

ways to live a simpler
and more spiritual life

Leave things undone

Besides the noble art of getting things done,
there is the noble art of leaving things undone.
The wisdom of life consists in the elimination of non-essentials.
Lin Yutang, author (1895–1976)

Time-management courses, hand-held electronic personal organizers
and pocket appointment calendars are symbols of a culture that gets a
lot done. If your definition of a successful life is getting a vast amount
done, then you've probably arrived. But of course the more important
question to ask yourself is, 'What exactly am I doing?'

After taking stock of your 'to do' list on a given day, ask yourself,
'What on this list is essential?' You may conclude that nothing can be
deleted. Then ask the deeper question, 'What on this list is truly
essential to my life and my happiness?' Begin to
question on a daily
basis what is really
essential and what isn't.
When you identify those
activities that are non-
essential, begin leaving
those things undone.

Do your own ghost-busting

In my definition there are four categories of clutter: things you do not use or love, things that are untidy or disorganized, too many things in too small a space and anything unfinished.

Karen Kingston, author of *Clear Your Clutter*

If you have a problem with clutter, you can be sure that it's serving some psychological purpose. Some objects can be particularly difficult to part with, even if you really don't want them around any longer. Those objects may represent 'ghosts' from your past.

It may be a threadbare sweater knitted by your late grandmother or some pottery your ex-boyfriend made. The problem is that living with objects that embody unresolved issues can drain your energy.

Write letters to each person involved. Tell them you love them very much, but it's time for you to stop holding on to the past. When you are ready, throw the objects away, sell them or donate them to charity.

Recognize things as they are

Things are as they are. Looking out into the universe at night, we make no comparisons between right and wrong stars, nor between well and badly arranged constellations.

Alan W. Watts, philosopher and author (1915–73)

One of the most profound ways to simplify your life is to stop wanting things and people to be different from the way they are.

If you give up judging and resisting, you may fear that you will become a doormat, without aspirations or strong emotions. But what you gain is a loving heart, from which you can deeply, compassionately and joyously engage with life.

Think of a difficult relationship in your life. Experience your resistance to whatever makes this relationship problematic. Then imagine letting go and accepting this person just as he or she is. Which state of mind feels better?

Take a Japanese bath

In the West, a bath is a place one goes to cleanse the body. In Japan, one goes there to cleanse the soul.

Bruce Smith and Yoshiko Yamamoto, authors of *The Japanese Bath*

Every evening without fail, millions of people lower themselves gently into the steaming waters of a Japanese bath. Whether it is a natural hot spring or a small tub at home, this daily ritual remains an integral part of Japanese life. With a little imagination, you too can add a deeply satisfying evening soak to your daily routine.

Start by cleaning the bath and putting away any bathroom clutter. Light some unscented candles. Shower with soap and rinse yourself; then fill your bath with hot water. Get in and sink down up to your neck. Just relax ... Vow to make time in your life for this ancient and exquisitely therapeutic pleasure.

Gaze at the stars

Be glad of life because it gives you a chance to love and to work and to play and to look up at stars.
Henry Vandyke, author and Presbyterian minister (1852–1933)

Throughout history the panoply of stars has drawn the eyes of humans skywards. We give them names, see pictures in their random placements and even navigate our world by their light.

But, in our citified ways, we live mostly indoors and, more often than not, get our experience of nature via our glowing TVs. If we do chance to look skywards, the glare of street lights may hide the awesome beauty above.

It's time to join your ancestors in a bit of star-gazing. Pick a clear night, grab a blanket and head for as dark an area as you can find. Let your mind flow among the patterns. Delight in the occasional shooting star or blinking satellite. Allow yourself to 'fall' into the vast night sky above.

Discover the noble bean

Have you noticed that simple things are often the most satisfying?
Deborah Taylor-Hough, author of *A Simple Choice*

Our food choices are dizzying, but unfortunately much of the food we buy is over-processed and unhealthy. Food bills take a considerable chunk of our pay cheque, and meats and poultry can form the biggest share.

Enter the much-maligned bean, once considered the food of 'peasants'. We now have nutrition experts and gourmet cooks having a love affair with the legume. Besides being incredibly delicious, beans are chock-full of vitamins, fibre and minerals, as well as omega-3 fatty acids and cancer-fighting phytochemicals.

Buy organic beans, either canned or dried. Be sure to sample a wide variety, from the elegant black bean to the Zen-like aduki. Explore cookbooks at your local library for healthy, inexpensive, gourmet bean recipes.

Cut down on sugar

We are recommending that you eat like your ancestors ate (until very recently), because they ate zero refined sugar and only whole-grain and unrefined foods.

H. Leighton Steward *et al.*, **authors of** ***The New Sugar Busters***

The World Health Organization advises us to limit our intake of sugar. Sugar consumption is at an all-time high, and more of us than ever before are overweight. Excessive sugar intake is a suspect in diseases such as diabetes and obesity.

If you want to cut down, avoid packaged foods that contain large amounts of sugar. Buy unsweetened cereals; drink 100 per cent fruit juices; choose sugary foods that have some nutritional value – such as oatmeal biscuits over sugary biscuits; eat fresh fruit for dessert.

Decide what you want to do before you die

To die is poignantly bitter, but the idea of having to die without having lived is unbearable.
Erich Fromm, psychologist (1900–80)

Do you create daily 'to do' lists? If so, great! This is an efficient way to negotiate your busy life and get things done. But what about your long-term vision? Have you lost track of what you really want to accomplish?

Try generating a different kind of 'to do' list. This one requires facing the inevitable: that one day you will no longer have your precious life. At first, it may seem an unpleasant task. However, by asking yourself what you want to do before you die, you easily and inevitably hone in on what matters most. Do you want to design and build your own house? Make peace with your brother? Set aside a special time and write down whatever comes to mind – don't wait to start doing what matters most.

Don't be a consumer

Is consuming the essence of who we are? It would seem not. For most of our existence we were makers, not consumers ...
Matthew Fox, spiritual theologian (b. 1940)

Shopping is part of our modern way of life. But it's important to remind yourself that you are not a consumer. Your importance as a human being is not measured by your buying power, or by the sophistication of your carefully researched choices. Your value is not measured by the cut of your clothes, by the car you drive or by the brand of anything you buy.

For one week, don't go shopping. Try creating something instead. You could plant your own herbs, write a poem, make a drawing or bake something from scratch. Let go of being a passive consumer and embrace yourself as a maker and a creative being.

Make peace with your financial past

Whatever you find, it's important to remember that net worth does not equal self-worth.
Joe Dominguez, author (1939–97)

If you're in debt, you're not alone. Or perhaps you've made a terrible financial mistake. Did you buy the wrong house, invest in the wrong stocks or spend your life savings on collecting something silly?

If you've not managed your money well in the past, admit it. Let go of the guilt and regret, because you'll need all that bound-up energy to repair the damage. You may want to examine your past financial life and see where you need to change. If you need help, don't hesitate to get psychological or financial counselling. Remember that money, like everything else, is a form of energy. Vow to explore a new relationship to money that is healthy and balanced – and one that serves your highest aims.

Use dreams for guidance

Both dreams and myths are important communications from ourselves to ourselves.

Erich Fromm, psychologist (1900–80)

Every night we have the opportunity to tap a goldmine. The goldmine is the world of our dreams. It's here that we can find guidance, learn about ourselves, solve problems and gain insights.

Before you go to sleep, set the intention to remember your dreams. Place a notebook and pen next to your bed, and in the morning write down everything you can recall. Do this for at least a week until you create the habit of remembering. Treat every aspect of the dream as a fascinating aspect of yourself. If a bird appears in your dream, be the bird. Or have a dialogue with the main person in your dream. Be open to both the positive and the negative, as your unconscious can be a tremendous resource for understanding your life. Let your dreams become an ally and a guide.

Practise kindness

Constant kindness can accomplish much. As the sun makes ice melt, kindness causes misunderstanding, mistrust and hostility to evaporate.
Albert Schweitzer, theologian, physician and missionary (1875–1965)

You may want to be kind, but you may have a habit of putting yourself first. An antidote to self-cherishing is to consider others to be as important as yourself. In doing so you are better able to respond appropriately to their needs. Practising kindness, then, becomes much easier and can even become a way of life.

On a daily basis, commit to at least one kind act each day. It could be as simple as giving a hug, sharing your home-grown tomatoes or calling a sick friend. If you want to take on kindness on a bigger scale, volunteer to work for a non-profit-making organization in your community. Practising kindness helps others and will make *you* happy as well.

Manage information

We're drowning in information and starving for knowledge.
**Rutherford D. Rogers, Yale University librarian, *New York Times*,
25 February 1985**

Your typical workday may start with wading through a hundred emails;
then on to voice mails, faxes, memos and manuals. At home, your cable
and satellite TV churns out news and entertainment for hours each day.
You can't possibly get to all the newspapers, magazines and books you
feel you need to read.

Instead of compulsively pursuing information, decide what you can
handle and limit yourself to what you can comfortably digest. Don't
answer every email. Let go of your fear that you are missing something
or being left behind. Remember that information should not be confused
with experience or knowledge. In other words, in addition to searching
the Internet for information on birds, be sure to go bird-watching.

Create true wealth

Wealth is the ability to fully experience life.

Henry David Thoreau, essayist, poet and naturalist (1817–62)

When we think of wealth, we usually think of material wealth, freedom from financial worry or a beautiful home. But this is not an adequate definition of true wealth. Money is just one element in a system that makes up a good life.

Make a list of all your non-financial assets. This could include your education, friends, job, health, spouse, family members and pets. Do you have a vision for your life and spiritual values? These intangibles are part of your wealth as well. Do you participate in various communities – religious, professional or recreational? These wonderful people enrich you with support and companionship. Do you enjoy the place in which you live? Do you partake of its amenities, such as parks and libraries? Generate a sense of gratitude for all aspects of your wealth.

Make healing soups

Soups are a good way to combine various ingredients and qualities for certain illnesses and temperaments.
Paul Pitchford, author of *Healing with Whole Foods*

Living a simpler life includes taking better care of yourself and your health. And the right foods can be good medicine.

Learn to make soups that boost your immune system and heal your ailments. Consult a good cookbook on how to make healing soups to aid a variety of health problems. You'll find recipes that detoxify your body, help you lose weight, cure your colds and enhance your immunity. When you don't feel well, home-made soup can be a great comfort, as well as a health-booster.

Rent things instead of buying them

If you're buying a tool you will only use briefly ... you may find it's better to rent.

Amy Dacyczyn, author of *The Complete Tightwad Gazette*

Some items that you rarely need or use are better rented than purchased. A table saw for making built-in shelves, a cement mixer for creating that new walkway, and folding chairs for your parents' 50th wedding anniversary are good candidates for rental. You can even rent dishes, silverware, VCRs or DVDs for special occasions.

Rent bicycles, ice skates, roller blades and skis. Rent a van for the holidays. Rent videos and make popcorn, instead of taking the whole family to the movies. You'll not only save money, but you'll have less stuff to clutter up your house and garage, and will spend less money on items that simply lose their value over time.

Distinguish between necessities and desires

Civilization is a limitless multiplication of unnecessary necessities.
Mark Twain, author (1835–1910)

Take a sheet of paper and write down what you feel are the very basic necessities of life. You may have on your list food, shelter, clothing, work, health care, and perhaps a partner or a spiritual life. Next, write down what you feel are the necessities of *your* life. By now – if you are like most other people – your list has probably expanded considerably. You may have written down: a certain standard of shelter, a certain amount of and style of clothing, and perhaps new furniture and a top-of-the-range computer.

After you've listed your necessities, go back over them. Consider each item and ask yourself if it is really a necessity or a desire. Do you have any unnecessary necessities on your list?

Go home

Home is where one starts from.

T. S. Eliot, poet (1888–1965)

Home can mean many things. We yearn to 'go home' – wherever that may be. We get 'homesick'. With some people we feel more 'at home' than with others. We want our house or apartment to 'feel like home'.

What does home mean to you? Do you feel at home in your body? Do you yearn to come home to yourself? Spend some time writing about what 'home' means to you. If you don't feel at home in your physical dwelling, in your job, your relationship or your city or town, ask why that is so. What changes do you need to make in order to feel at home in your body, your mind and your physical surroundings?

Nourish your friendships

Close friends contribute to our personal growth. They also contribute to our personal pleasure, making the music sound sweeter, the wine taste richer, the laughter ring louder because they are there.
Judith Viorst, novelist and poet (b. 1931)

Our friendships can be the most nourishing and sustaining relationships of our lives. Yet our cultures often rank our marriage partner, our parents or our siblings as more important. Without thinking, we can subtly devalue our friendships when they may, in fact, be the most crucial ingredient in our sense of well-being and happiness.

Make a list of those people in your life whom you consider to be friends. Do you sometimes feel more intimate with your friends than with anyone else in your life? Honour them by letting them know how much they mean to you. Nourish your friendships by making time for friends in your life.

Celebrate festivals meaningfully

Each holiday, with its unique history and set of rituals, connected the members of a community to one another, and to the community's collective past.

Barry Schwartz, psychologist and educationalist (b. 1946)

Was your last festival or holiday a disappointment? If you celebrate Christmas, Hanukkah or Kwanzaa, was the experience more stressful than enjoyable? Were you disappointed in the emphasis on gifts or in the quality of time spent with family and friends? Did the spiritual significance of the occasion get lost in the commercial hype?

For your next festival, think about what it means to you and why you want to celebrate it. Plan it in a conscious way. Talk about the event ahead of time with family and friends. On the day of the celebration, ask everyone present to share what the day means to them.

Get rid of guilt

Guilt agonizes over trifles, ignores wrongdoing.
Mason Cooley, aphorist (b. 1927)

Guilt is a useless emotion. You can become stuck in guilt and shame, and even make it part of your identity. Yet it doesn't necessarily lead you to change your behaviour or make you a better person. Regret, on the other hand, is a more positive emotion. It allows you to focus on your actions, and moves you towards change and healing.

First, if you caused someone harm, acknowledge it. Then express sincere regret for having hurt them. Let them know this is not the way you want to behave. If possible, do something to make amends. Ask the person what you can do to make things better. And then commit to yourself, and to them, that you will refrain from that harmful behaviour in future. Allow yourself to feel purified and renewed by this process.

Create a garden for your soul

I know a little garden-close, set thick with lily and red rose,
where I would wander if I might from dewy dawn to dewy night.
William Morris, poet (1834–96)

You can plant flowers or tomatoes, mow the lawn and get your ivy to climb. Gardening can be just another weekend chore – or it can feed your soul and your imagination.

Assess the state of your garden – whether it's a few clay pots on a balcony or a generous expanse behind your house. What would make your garden magical, whimsical and a delight to your soul? Is it colour, fragrance, places to walk and shady places to meditate? Or is it herbs and vegetables, which have personalities of their own? If you are going to take the time and expense to make a garden, then have a relationship with its inhabitants and enjoy its spirit. Tend it lovingly and use it to soothe your soul. Make it a sacred place for joy, peace and prayer.

Remember to rest

Everywhere I have sought rest and not found it, except sitting in a corner by myself with a little book.
Thomas à Kempis, monk and mystic (1380–1471)

You've heard it often: that it's important to rest. You'll get to rest, you say, if there's time to rest. But ignore the need for rest at your peril. For it is by resting that you rejuvenate your body and mind.

During rest you may have your best insights and gain perspective on the frantic activity that has become the norm of modern life. Rest is essential to all creatures and all activities. It is integral to a musical score, a painting or a performance. In art there is always the play of movement and non-movement, activity and non-activity. The places of rest define and illuminate.

Do you get enough rest? Do you value rest as much as you do activity? How would your life change if you did so? After reading this, close your eyes and take a nap.

Meditate on your breath

Through meditation and by giving full attention to one thing at a time, we can learn to direct attention where we choose.
Eknath Easwaran, spiritual teacher (1910–99)

Meditation on the breath is an ancient method to calm the mind. To begin, sit cross-legged on a cushion or, if that's not possible, on a chair. Keep your spine straight and, if you're sitting on a chair, keep both feet flat on the floor. Cradle your right hand in your left and rest both loosely against your navel. Focus your eyes about 1m (3ft) in front of you.

Now pay attention to your breath as it enters and leaves your nostrils. Count your breaths up to ten, using the out-breath, then start again. Acknowledge any thoughts that arise and return immediately to your breath. Do this for ten minutes. Notice how often your mind strays from attention on your breath. Did you realize your mind was so active? Is there a pattern to your thoughts?

Write a love letter

I am a little pencil in the hand of a writing God who is sending a love letter to the world.

Mother Teresa, Catholic nun (1910–97)

This love letter is not for seduction, or attraction, or control. It is for expressing your love selflessly, without any strings attached. It is for telling someone how much you want them to be happy, how much you admire and appreciate who they are, and how grateful you are to know and love them. You can write this kind of love letter to anyone. It might be to your spouse, your mother, your father or one of your kids. It might be to a friend or a teacher. If you are not ready to express your love openly, write it but don't send it.

Expressing love in this way is freeing and nurturing – both for you and the other person. No emails, please. Use beautiful stationery and send it by post.

Dress from the inside out

I see that fashion wears out more apparel than the man.

William Shakespeare, dramatist and poet (1564–1616)

We are social animals. We want to fit in, be attractive and be seen as successful and powerful. The fashion industry makes plenty of money from our needs by dictating what clothes are 'in' during a given season, and promptly changing them the next.

Instead of trying to be *au courant*, try dressing from the inside out. For one week, wear only what you want to wear. Decide what (if anything) you want your clothing to say to the world. Pay attention to textures, and to the way your clothes feel against your body. What colours do you long to wear? If its fire-engine red, go for it! What styles do you like, regardless of what the fashion world is saying? Wear your clothes to express yourself. Use your clothing for rituals, for celebration and even for healing.

Look for the open door

When one door of happiness closes, another opens; but we look so long at the closed door that we do not see the one that has been opened for us.
Helen Keller, deaf-and-blind writer (1880–1968)

When a relationship ends, or you lose the job you love, or you don't get that scholarship, it's easy to get stuck in disappointment. Unfortunately, while you're staring at the closed door, you're missing the new ones that are constantly opening all around you.

One way not to get stuck is to ritually say goodbye when happiness leaves you. Write a letter and bid farewell. Then sit quietly and mentally release the person or situation you just lost. Go for a long walk and, with each step, see yourself moving on to new opportunities. They may not be what you expect, so be sure to stay open and positive for what the future may bring.

Use the Web mindfully

You affect the world by what you browse.

Tim Berners-Lee, inventor of the World Wide Web (b. 1955)

The World Wide Web and its big cousin, the Internet, create a world of extraordinary connections. What you choose to browse, and where you surf to on the Web, helps create the Web itself. If you set up your own site, you're offering it to hundreds of millions of Web users.

Because the Web is one big dynamic universe, it's important to keep your energy positive. Don't surf to negative websites, and don't create them, either. Be mindful of the quality of your communications. Energetically, you're now connected to millions of people around the world, so be careful how you contribute to that universe.

Give without strings

I have found that among its other benefits, giving liberates the soul of the giver.

Maya Angelou, poet (b. 1928)

Giving without strings is very liberating; giving *with* strings creates difficulties and misunderstandings. What usually gets in the way of open-hearted giving is the notion that you are entitled to something in return.

Before you give anything, ask yourself why you are giving it? Do you expect a similar monetary or material gift in return? Is it recognition, love, loyalty, ownership or even sex that you're expecting? Try to discover any 'strings' lurking in your motivation. Then mentally untie them from your gift. Now, if you are able, give your gift freely and lovingly, without reservation. In this way you can transform your giving into an opportunity for personal and spiritual growth.

Appreciate what you have

Think not on what you lack as much as on what you have.

Greek proverb

The trick to having a positive mind, even in the worst of times, is to focus on what's going right for you. When you feel you don't have everything you need, it's easy to discount your blessings. When you don't have money for the rent, and the bills are piling up – even though it may be difficult – focus on what you *do* have. Be sure to consider non-material wealth: your family and friends, your health, your education, your talents and your values. Then focus on the material wealth you do have (however small).

Even if you are wealthy, it's easy to focus on what you don't have. Regardless of your situation, always appreciate what you do have. This positive outlook will transform your life.

Practise Buddha's patience

Anger kills both laughter and joy; what greater foe is there than anger?
Tiruvalluvar, sage and poet (c. 5th century CE)

We think of patience as a willingness to wait for someone or something.
It's a patient person who sits peacefully at the airport waiting for you
to pick them up — an hour after you said you would meet them. Yet, in
the Buddha's teaching, patience is less about waiting and more about
actively controlling negative emotions, such as anger and hatred.
In order to develop patience in the face of your anger, try
these antidotes. When someone makes you angry, instead
of flying off the handle, try counting to ten. Or consider
that, just like you, they want to be happy and avoid
suffering. Allow yourself to soften by understanding
that they have the same motivation as you. Let go of
unrealistic expectations about how they *should* act.
Be open to working with the person to change
the situation that is making you angry.

Keep a journal

*I am carrying out my plan, so long formulated, of keeping a journal ...
and thus I shall improve myself.*
Eugène Delacroix, artist (1798–1863)

One of the best ways to help yourself is to write in a journal on a daily
basis. Try writing down your thoughts and feelings about whatever is
bothering you.

If you're having trouble with a friend or a spouse, use your journal to
explore the issues. Attempt to understand their perspective by writing
from their point of view. If you have to make a big decision, write down
the pros and cons and further explore your thoughts. If you want to
savour a special moment, record it in your journal. If you have spiritual
insights, express them. Try writing your journal first thing in the morning.
Articulating what's in and on your mind should free you to get on with
your day.

Learn to listen

It is the disease of not listening, the malady of not marking, that I am troubled with.

William Shakespeare, dramatist and poet (1564–1616)

Here's an old joke: in Hollywood, there are only two things – talking and waiting to talk. You may not be a movie star, but you too may have trouble listening. It takes effort to listen. More to the point, it takes an open mind and heart. That may be difficult for you to achieve. You may have a hard time trusting and want to protect yourself. Or perhaps no one listened to you when you were a child. However, through active listening, you gain the joy of deep communication with another human being. You may learn something valuable. And you may help someone to speak the truth. Practise the art of listening by focusing your attention on the other person. Before you respond, let them know you have heard and understood what they've said.

Practise voluntary simplicity

At the heart of a simple life is an emphasis on harmonious and purposeful living.

Duane Elgin, author of *Voluntary Simplicity*

Life in modern cities can feel overwhelmingly complicated and stressful. You're not alone if you work long hours, feel the pressure to get ahead and lose sleep over your mounting debt. You may have too little time with family and friends. A simpler life sounds like a good idea, yet you can't see the alternatives. Not participating in the 'rat race' means that you lose the race.

Are you living your life in alignment with your deepest values? You may need to backtrack and ask yourself, 'What *are* my deepest values?' Simplifying your life is a process that begins by asking the right questions. By asking the right questions, you may end up questioning the 'rat race' itself. At this point many alternatives may present themselves when before there seemed none.

Take your own lunch

There is no such thing as a free lunch.

Anonymous

Do you buy your lunch every day at work? If you do, you could be making a significant hole in your pay cheque. Of course, there are lots of reasons to do this; such as: 'Who has time to make lunch in the morning?'; 'My friends go out to lunch and I don't want to be anti-social'; and 'It's not hip to bring a lunch box to work.'

Add up what you spend on lunches in a year. You may be in for a shock! How many hours did you work to pay for that daily expense? Now calculate how much it would cost to pack a simple lunch. Figure out the difference. How would you spend the money you would save? How about a holiday at the beach, or maybe a new computer?

Declare your interdependence

I am a part of all that I have met.
Alfred, Lord Tennyson, poet (1809–92)

If you are feeling alienated and alone, try meditating on the interdependence of all life. Consider that you are connected to all other living beings. You depend on others in countless ways and they depend on you. For instance, you depend on others to provide heat, light, electricity, health care, food, transportation, clothing, education, work, love and friendship – the list is endless. And you serve others in the same ways. You are also connected to all other sentient beings, and to all aspects of nature, both animate and inanimate.

You also depend on what you create with, and among, others. So your well-being – and the well-being of all – depends on your ability to create relationships that are balanced, loving and positive.

Express gratitude

The best way to show gratitude to God and to the people is to accept everything with joy.
Mother Teresa, Catholic nun (1910–97)

There is no better antidote to dissatisfaction than generating sincere gratitude for what you have. This is best done on a daily basis. The beauty of this practice is that you never run out of things to be thankful for.

Here are some ideas. Start by writing down a list of everyone in your life who has ever helped you. This should take quite a while. Write how you feel about the enormous amount of love and assistance you've received to date. Now write down everything you own. You will soon tire of doing this, but you'll quickly get the message. Compared to most people on the planet, you're unbelievably blessed.

Simplify your wardrobe

Simplicity, simplicity, simplicity!
Henry David Thoreau, essayist, poet and naturalist (1817–62)

If you work in an office, you probably have to look good every day, and this can consume your hard-earned money. If your clothing budget is eating into your salary, first consider having a simpler wardrobe.

Classic styles in solid colours can help you look presentable for work in half the time, and they last from season to season. If you have tops and bottoms that mix and match, you'll make a few pieces go a long way. Be sure to buy khaki, black and white, and then build from there. Women: use scarves and jewellery to change your look. Men: use ties and coloured shirts. Also, try buying women's or men's business suits at a secondhand clothing shop. The cost savings are significant.

Fight obesity

Never eat more than you can lift.
Miss Piggy, character on *The Muppets* TV show

Miss Piggy's comment was meant to be funny. But health researchers are alarmed at the growing rate of obesity. So why is this occurring? One cause may be the over-abundance of processed foods in our diet; another may be the fast-food restaurants that are now found worldwide.

Maybe it's due to sugar and white flour consumption having increased at a staggering rate in the last century.

Are you at a healthy weight? Do you need to shed some pounds? If so, take a hard look at what you eat, and learn about good nutrition. Simplify your diet so that it includes only fresh, whole foods.

Work with joy

And no one shall work for money, and no one shall work for fame,
but each for the joy of the working.
Rudyard Kipling, writer and poet (1865–1936)

We work primarily for an income. Yet we also work for the approval of others, for a sense of power and mastery, and to be of service to others. But how many of us work to experience joy? It's not so much what you do as *how* you do it that's the key to joyful work.

Be fully present, at each moment, as you go through your day. You can do this by bringing all your senses and awareness to each task. In other words, regardless of pressure, focus only on what you are doing now. By doing so you'll be less reactive to external demands and interruptions, and more empowered in using your skills and knowledge. You'll also unleash your creativity and problem-solving abilities.

Wake up to time

Time is a sort of river of passing events, and strong is its current.
Marcus Aurelius, Roman emperor (121–80 CE)

You wear a watch to keep on schedule. You may buy books on time management. And complain that you're so busy you just don't have enough time in the day. You say, 'I need to find more time' or 'I need to make more time'. This suggests you have the power to create more of it whenever you need it. But do you really understand the dynamic quality of time?

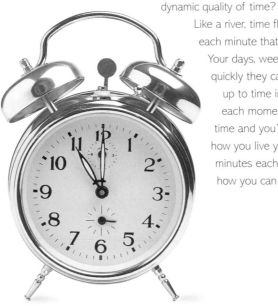

Like a river, time flows on relentlessly, and each minute that passes is irreplaceable. Your days, weeks and months pass so quickly they can seem like a dream. Wake up to time in order to experience that each moment is precious. Wake up to time and you'll make better choices in how you live your life. Spend a few minutes each morning meditating on how you can best use your time today.

Say grace

Expressing gratitude for the food on our table is universal.

Sarah McElwain, author of *Saying Grace*

Whether or not you practise a religion, consider 'saying grace' before your meals. Saying grace expresses gratitude for what you are about to eat, in the form of a prayer. You can thank God or a higher power, or simply thank the universe for giving you the food you are about to enjoy. You can thank the farmer who planted it, the workers who harvested it, the grocer who sold it and (if not yourself) the person who prepared it.

Saying grace can remind you of your connection and indebtedness to all other living beings. It can even help you be mindful of the quality and amount of the food you eat. Try saying grace before every meal — with friends, family, when alone or at work.

Practise centring prayer

If you think of prayer as just words or songs, it's very limited. Prayer is primarily, in essence, a relationship.

Father Thomas Keating, author of *Contemplative Prayer*

Most religious traditions practise some form of centring prayer. You can create your own, based on the Christian tradition.

Start with a spiritual text that inspires you. Allow a word to emerge from your reading that resonates within you. For example, try God, Buddha, Jesus, Love or Peace. This sacred word expresses your intent for God or the Sacred to enter your heart and be present in your life.

Sit comfortably with your eyes closed and introduce your word inwardly. When you become aware of thoughts or distractions, bring yourself back to your sacred word. Do this for 20 minutes. At the end of your prayer, remain silent with your eyes closed for a few more minutes. Notice the effects of centring prayer on your daily life.

Rejoice in the face of envy

Difficult people are, as usual, the greatest teachers.
Pema Chödrön, Buddhist nun (b. 1936)

Rejoicing in everyday things is a powerful practice. When we drop our chronic dissatisfaction and find joy in simple pleasures – a beautiful rose, the smell of bread baking, the laughter of a child – it uplifts us.

An extension of this practice is rejoicing in the good fortune of others. It's fairly easy to celebrate a loved one's accomplishments. However, when you have difficulty with someone, you may have a hard time enjoying their successes. You may say 'Congratulations!', but in your heart your words ring hollow. Examine the stories you are telling yourself. Do you wish the other person failure at the same time as you're feeling inadequate? Notice how jealousy and envy hurt you, and cause you misery. Experiment with rejoicing in the face of your envy, and notice how it frees your heart and eases your own suffering.

Explore mentoring

A mentor's principal purpose is to help another develop the qualities he or she needs to attain his or her goals – without a mentor.
Shirley Peddy, author of *The Art of Mentoring*

Mentoring is a way to give and get life counselling. You can mentor a person by giving support, counsel, friendship and constructive example. Or you can have a mentor yourself. If you're trying to excel in a particular career, having a mentor can make all the difference.

Identify someone who is accomplished in something you want to do. Approach him or her for advice and counsel. If you both like each other, ask that the relationship be ongoing. If you want to be a mentor for a young person, search on the Web for organizations in your area that work with kids. Mentoring is a wonderful way to give to your community.

Recognize impermanence

Oh this is the joy of the rose, that it blows and goes.
Willa Cather, novelist (1873–1947)

Nothing lasts. When you ignore this fact, you cause yourself to suffer.
You may cling to things that are transient, like fame and fortune, and be
shocked when a friend or family member dies. It's especially hard to
comprehend your own inevitable death.

But consider that, without impermanence, a flower wouldn't blossom,
the rain wouldn't fall, the sun wouldn't rise in the morning or set in the
evening. The tragedies of today would not give way to the blessings of
tomorrow. There would be no hope, no healing, no future.

Try meditating on the reality of impermanence. Think about your life
a year ago and how you have changed for better or worse since
then. An understanding of impermanence can bring
perspective to any situation.

Make a budget

The budget should be balanced.
Marcus Tullius Cicero, orator and statesman (106–43 BC)

Why make a budget? You may feel that you don't make enough money to make this worthwhile. But the less you have, the more you need a budget. If you're in debt and without savings, you definitely need one.

First, track your expenses for three months. When you have a picture of where your money is going, decide where you can cut back. Second, list all your debts. Third, create a budget for the next year by calculating your income and your fixed and variable expenses. Design your budget with relevant categories. Fourth, track your income and expenses and keep your budget up-to-date.

A budget is a financial tool for getting out of debt and increasing your financial wealth. It's also a tool for living a more conscious and balanced life.

Stay spiritually empowered

*To be inspired is to be moved in an extraordinary manner by the power
or Spirit of God to act, speak or think what is holy, just and true.*
Henry More, philosopher (1614–87)

Your spiritual life – however you define it – helps you find meaning in
your life. But, without effort to keep yourself inspired, your spiritual life
can become lifeless. Of course, one antidote to a flagging spiritual life is
to pray, meditate and read uplifting material.

But there is much more you can do. For true inspiration, try bringing
the wisdom of God, Spirit or your higher power to every moment in your
life. When you talk to a colleague, see the divine in him or her. When you

watch a movie, bring your
spiritual understanding to the
story unfolding in front of you.
When you watch the evening
news, allow yourself to feel
compassion for the people
and events you witness.

Go on a nature walk

The day I see a leaf is a marvel of a day.
Kenneth Patton, Christian minister and poet (1911–94)

Unless your job takes you outside, you probably spend a lot of time working and living indoors. But don't let your busy schedule deprive you of walking amid nature.

Check out what parks are available nearby. If you have a little more time, try to get out of the city. Give yourself at least an hour to walk in a garden or wooded area. When walking, try not to get lost in your thoughts. Instead, focus on your surroundings. Pay attention to the trees, the plants and flowers. How many can you name? Notice any animals, birds and insects, and examine their behaviour. Breathe deeply and experience the heady smells of the earth. Nature walks renew body and soul and are a great activity to share with children.

Pray for the Earth

It is a wholesome and necessary thing for us to turn again to the earth and in the contemplation of her beauties to know of wonder and humility.

Rachel Carson, environmentalist and author (1907–64)

It's no surprise that the Earth suffers from our living on it. We pollute her skies, her oceans, her rivers and her ground. Our human activities cause global warming and even put holes in the ozone layer. Because of these sad realities, you may be inspired to donate money or volunteer your time for environmental causes. But don't forget the power of prayer.

Take a moment to pray every day for our beautiful planet. Pray for the Earth because our health and survival depend on her. Praying for the Earth will help calm any anger or fear you may be experiencing and restore your optimism and hope.

Use stress-busters

Every stress leaves an indelible scar.
Hans Selye, physician and author (1907–82)

Stress takes its toll on our bodies and minds. So what can you do to counteract its effects? First of all, whatever you do, do it on a daily basis. Meditating or walking once a month isn't going to help. Second, spend a month exploring many different methods of stress reduction so that you can find out what works for you.

Are you a movement person? Then try walking, biking or t'ai chi. Are you an exercise type? Then go for yoga. Do you love music? Then listen to one of the many music CDs made for relaxation; or, if you find voices soothing, try listening to a recorded guided meditation. If you need quiet, then find somewhere you can experience complete silence for 15 or 30 minutes each day. If you need self-expression, try painting, singing, writing or dancing.

Calculate the true cost of our job

Knowing the financial bottom line for your job will help to clarify further your motives for working and for selecting one job over another.
Joe Dominguez and Vicki Robin, authors of *Your Money or Your Life*

To assess how much money you're really making, it's important to look at the hidden costs of maintaining your job. Hidden job-related expenses are: commuting, which costs both time *and* money; daycare and after-school care; clothing and dry cleaning; make-up and hair styling; time spent getting ready for work; lunches, coffee and snacks; time spent unwinding after work; job-related illnesses; expensive holidays to get away from work; work-related books, education and conferences; house cleaning, gardening and other services.

Now add up your real hours worked and your *real* hourly wage. Is your job taking too much of your life energy?

Pray for peace

Peace puts forth her olive everywhere.

William Shakespeare, dramatist and poet (1564–1616)

News reports of war and conflict are stressful and take their toll on your daily health and well-being. You may feel powerless to do anything in the face of such human suffering. However, one thing you can do is pray for those involved.

Close your eyes and sit quietly for a moment. Bring to mind a part of the world that is experiencing violence and upheaval. Do not take sides. Instead, simply pray that those living through this turmoil find a peaceful way to solve their differences. Pray that they heal their hearts of anger and blame, and find a compromise that will restore peace. Pray for all the children harmed and killed in war. Join with many others around the world in praying for peace on a daily basis.

Eat in

I was 32 when I started cooking; up until then, I just ate.
Julia Child, cook and author (b. 1912)

If you want to save some serious money, stop 'eating out' in restaurants. Instead, buy groceries and 'eat in'. If that sounds like a prison sentence, you may want to explore some of the positive reasons for cooking and eating at home.

First, you'll learn how to cook or be a better cook. Use your local library as a source of free cookbooks. Second, you can improve your health by controlling what and how much you eat. No more greasy fast food or huge restaurant portions. Third, you can enjoy gourmet meals without breaking the bank – recreate those special dishes at home. Fourth, you can enjoy low-cost socializing with friends by having pot-luck meals. Fifth, you can potentially save lots of money per year. Now, what's so bad about that?

Keep track of everything you spend

We're afraid to look at our finances head-on, to see where everything really goes.

Suze Orman, author of *The 9 Steps to Financial Freedom*

This may sound unbelievably tedious. However, it's the best exercise possible for getting a grip on your financial life.

Once you get into the habit, it's simple. Keep all receipts and put them in a drawer or large envelope. Once a week, record everything you've spent, according to categories that make sense to you. You can do this in a ledger or on your computer. After a few months you'll have a perfect snapshot of where your hard-earned money goes. Did you discover large categories for CDs, coffee or entertainment? Are you eating out way too much? You now have the information to enable you to decide if you really want to spend your life energy working for what you've been buying.

Heal through prayer

There is overwhelming evidence that if you take prayer into the laboratory and subject it to testing you can show that it works.
Larry Dossey, author of *Healing Words*

Scientific studies show that prayer can affect healing in positive ways. It doesn't matter if you believe in a higher power or not; your prayer can enhance healing in yourself or others, and can be effective over long distances as well.

If you're suffering from an illness, try invoking God or a higher power, and ask for his or her help in healing. Or simply send out your request for healing to the entire universe. Visualize healing energies returning to you in the form of a beautiful golden light. Let the light fill your body. Imagine, with your whole heart, that you are healed. You can also pray in this way for someone else.

Become a tightwad

Diligence is the basis of wealth, and thrift the source of riches.
Chinese proverb

Thrift is a virtue that your great-grandparents admired. However, if you practise thrift today, you're often called a 'miser' or a 'tightwad'. You may think such people are unpleasant and cheerless, like Ebenezer Scrooge. More often, however, they're happy and content, because they're in control of their finances. Maybe they have a secret you don't know.

Explore the many websites on the Internet dedicated to frugal living. Sign up for free newsletters from veteran tightwads, and enjoy endless tips on how to save money and conserve resources. Learn how to make a pack of aluminium foil last a year! You may roll your eyes, but while you're drowning in debt misers are living stress-free, with clear goals and purpose. While you can't make ends meet, they have money in the bank and a lot of leisure time. Consider becoming a tightwad yourself.

Eat frugally and deliciously

*To live content with small means; to seek elegance rather than luxury ...
this is my symphony.*

William Henry Channing, minister (1810–84)

Because our grocery shops offer us a dizzying array of foods, it can be difficult to keep from over-spending. You may be padding your food bill with gourmet treats, convenience foods and expensive cuts of meat. How can you reduce your grocery budget and still have great-tasting home-cooked meals? The solution is to learn about low-cost healthy foods and practise discipline when you are at the supermarket.

Start by giving up most packaged foods. Buy fresh or in bulk whenever possible. There are hundreds of cookbooks devoted to 'frugal food'. Use them to identify economical ingredients and mouthwatering recipes, without sacrificing quality and taste. Find recipes for inexpensive cuts of meat, bean dishes, home-made breads and baked goods. When you shop, make a list and stick to it.

Be truthful

The good I stand on is my truth and honesty.

William Shakespeare, dramatist and poet (1564–1616)

One of the best ways to simplify your life is to be honest. There's nothing more stressful than keeping track of stories you've invented or embellished. It may seem like a good idea, at the time, to alter the truth – you may want to protect someone from pain, or protect yourself from embarrassment; or maybe you're intending to give yourself an advantage and cheat in a test.

But, in the long run, if you are dishonest you complicate your life. And in the end you may cause more pain to yourself and others than if you had told the truth. Honesty is like a fresh breeze. The trick is to be simultaneously honest and kind.

Redefine success

Success is an absurd, erratic thing.

Alice Foote MacDougall, businesswoman (1867–1945)

Our culture's definition of success is fairly limited. The signs are mostly external: a high-paying job, a nice car, beautiful clothes, a beautiful partner and a large home.

Consider these alternative definitions of success, which don't require conspicuous consumption: you have a successful life if you have a safe place to live, good health, a nurturing family life, ongoing education, spiritual development, good friends, and work that feeds you emotionally and intellectually. You're a successful person if you are capable of giving and receiving love and experiencing joy.

What do you consider to be the ingredients of a successful life? More importantly, how do you measure success for yourself?

Make an income and expense chart

You may find ... that you can come up with wonderfully creative ways to trim your spending so that you hardly notice.

Suze Orman, author of *The 9 Steps to Financial Freedom*

If you want to live a simpler life, start by spending less money. If you spend less money, you won't have to work as hard. If you're very frugal and save a lot, you may end up not having to work much at all. What will you do with all that wonderful free time?

Get a large sheet of graph paper and start tracking your income and expenses. Post this chart on a wall where it is visible to your whole family. Find creative ways to cut your spending. Watch your expense line go down and your savings increase. Use your wall chart for reinforcement, fun and inspiration on your journey to a less stressful, simpler and more spiritual life.

Have a spiritual New Year's Eve

The object of a new year is not that we should have a new year. It is that we should have a new soul.

G. K. Chesterton, author and critic (1874–1936)

All cultures celebrate New Year's Eve. It's a great time to have a party, send out the old and bring in the new. For a change of pace, invite some close friends and family to your home for a New Year's Eve ritual.

Start with a festive pot-luck meal. Then sit around the fire or light candles. Have someone offer a prayer of intention that this ritual strengthen and encourage everyone present. Begin with each person sharing their gratitude for the passing year. If anyone experienced tragedies or hardships, let them express their sorrow for what they endured. End with everyone outlining their hopes and resolutions. At midnight, hold hands in a moment of silence. Pray for peace and happiness in the coming year. Then break out the champagne!

Simplify your kitchen

If you can organize your kitchen you can organize your life.

Louis Parrish, author of *Cooking as Therapy*

Your kitchen can quickly become overwhelmed with clutter. Over time, it's easy to collect utensils you don't use, food that's out of date and dishes that have never seen the light of your table. Having a clean, organized and efficient kitchen will encourage you to cook meals at home and save you money.

Start by emptying all your kitchen cabinets and drawers. Sort your dishes, pots, pans and utensils into piles – those that you want to keep, those that are broken or excessively worn and those that you can give to charity. Next, sort through your staples and condiments. Throw out the old stuff, including old spices. Get rid of any appliances you don't use. Finally, clean your cabinets inside and out and put back everything you want to keep.

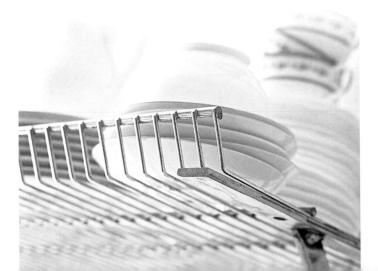

Get some sunlight

Be like the flower, turn your faces to the sun.
Kahlil Gibran, poet and philosopher (1883–1931)

Sunlight is one of the most overlooked keys to good health. Unfortunately, too much living indoors, coupled with a fear of skin cancer, has kept us from enjoying its benefits.

Excessive exposure to the sun may cause skin cancer, but there is also evidence that sunlight helps prevent other forms of cancer, as well as heart disease and osteoporosis. Sunlight benefits your bones, lowers your cholesterol and blood pressure and wards off depression. Our bodies need 400 units of vitamin D a day – you can get that by exposing your face to sunlight for 15 minutes. We all feel better when the sun comes out. For better health, be sure to get a little sunlight each day.

Meditate on loving kindness

Loving-kindness for oneself is the golden key to appreciating other people, even the ones that drive you crazy.
Pema Chödrön, Buddhist nun (b. 1936)

Loving-kindness meditation helps you bring love and kindness into your consciousness, so that you can bring it into your daily life.

Sit in your usual meditation posture and centre yourself with your breath. Visualize the love and acceptance of God or a higher power surrounding you and entering your body. Let go of any self-hatred you may be harbouring. Feel the love and acceptance filling your heart.

Now turn your attention to those you love. Imagine love and kindness flowing to them in the form of white light. Next, turn your attention to those with whom you have difficulties. See them bathed in the warmth of love and kindness. Then imagine all other beings bathed in love and acceptance.

Drink water

It is essential for the proper functioning of the body to drink at least eight glasses of quality water each day.

James F. Balch, MD, author of *Prescription for Nutritional Healing*

Water is simplicity itself. And our bodies are two-thirds water; the human brain is 95 per cent water, blood is 82 per cent water and the lungs are nearly 90 per cent water. So adequate water benefits nearly every human body function.

The benefits of drinking enough water are extensive, so it is worth mentioning a few. Water removes toxins from the body and helps with elimination. It aids digestion and converting food into energy. It helps you lose weight, have more energy and perform better. Staying fully hydrated reduces headaches and dizziness. Drinking adequate water decreases your chances of getting colon and bladder cancer. And there are beauty benefits: your skin looks fresher and younger. If you're addicted to sugary soft drinks, try pure water as a healthy alternative.

Exercise cheaply

Health is the vital principle of bliss, and exercise, of health.

James Thomson, poet (1700–48)

Gym and health-club memberships are expensive. It just takes a little thought and creativity to find an alternative.

Some suggestions are: ride your bicycle to work; walk short distances instead of driving; use the stairs instead of elevators; or do some gardening as a form of exercise. Check out your neighbourhood parks for walking and running tracks – some of them include stations for doing chin-ups or other exercises. And inexpensive exercise balls are great for home use. They help you improve your balance, coordination and core strength in your abdominals and back. If you want company when you exercise, check your local newspaper for details of walking, running and biking clubs.

Stay in a hostel

The world is a book, and those who do not travel, read only a page.
St Augustine of Hippo, theologian (354–430 CE)

If you've given up holidays because of the high cost of hotel rooms, try hostelling. Hostels used to be for young people, but now travellers of all ages can enjoy this low-cost accommodation all over the world. Hostels vary widely, so it's best to do your homework before you leave home. Try researching on the Internet or buying a hostel guide for the country you plan to visit.

Some hostels offer everything from dorm rooms to single rooms. Bathrooms may be shared or private. Most hostels include shared living space, such as kitchens, common rooms and meeting areas, which provide an opportunity to get to know travellers from other countries. Make reservations ahead if possible, especially in the summer months. Bring a lock for your suitcase or backpack. And ask beforehand if you need to bring your own towels and bed linen.

Practise silence

No spiritual exercise is as good as that of silence.
Seraphim of Sarov, Orthodox Christian saint (1759–1833)

Find a way to be alone in a quiet place. Take a vow of silence for the next 24 hours. Don't speak a word or communicate with anyone in any way. Don't watch television or listen to your radio or CD player. Stay away from your computer, and unplug the phone and your bleeper. Turn off your mobile phone too. Do not read for distraction or entertainment.

Use this time to meditate, do yoga or take a bath. Write about silence and solitude and how they make you feel. Are you comfortable being alone without your normal distractions? Are you scared, bored, anxious or relieved? Do you find the silence nurturing and renewing? Let the silence provide an opening to explore the most fragile and tender parts of your soul.

Breathe deeply

T'is the breathing time of day with me.
William Shakespeare, dramatist and poet (1564–1616)

Because of the stress and tension inherent in our modern way of life,
we have a habit of not breathing deeply. It's amazing that many of us
don't keel over on the pavement, blue in the face from lack of oxygen!
Notice when you tend to suppress your breathing. Is it when you are
feeling tense, angry or afraid? Or is it when you're concentrating intently
on your work?

Take time often during your day to breathe deeply. Breathe into
whatever part of your body is tense or in pain. Use your breath often to
calm yourself and to balance your emotions. Over time, your physical
health will improve as a result.

Turn off the TV

Television should be kept in its proper place – beside us, before us, but never between us and the larger life.
Robert Fraser, head of the British Independent Television Authority, 1958

Television has its redeeming values, but mostly it bombards us with images of conflict, violence and exploitation. Like moths drawn to the light, we sit mesmerized in front of the screen. The problem is: not only do our minds become dulled by the constant stimulation, but we begin to confuse this passive, vicarious activity with actual living.

Like most addictions, a TV addiction can be hard to kick. Try cutting down gradually by substituting other activities that you find enjoyable. Have a family game night, take the dog for a walk in the park or read a book. Have days with no television. Limit your viewing time and intentionally choose what you want to watch.

Start something new

Age is something that doesn't matter, unless you are a cheese.
Billie Burke, actress (1885–1970)

Do you feel you're too old to start something new? Do you feel life has passed you by? Think again! American primitive artist Grandma Moses taught herself to paint in her late seventies. Selma Plaut earned her Bachelor's degree from the University of Toronto at the age of 100. George Dawson learned to read and write at 98, and wrote his autobiography, *Life Is So Good*, at 100. Tom Lane started swimming competitively at the age of 82. Centenarian comedians Bob Hope and George Burns kept us laughing until the end.

If you too want to live to be 100, accept change gracefully. Be a lifelong learner. Practise seeing the glass half full, and be eager to see what tomorrow brings. Most importantly, make new friends. No matter what your age, never stop pursuing your dreams.

Heal with music

Music is the answer to the mystery of life.

Arthur Schopenhauer, philosopher (1788–1850)

Music author and visionary Don Campbell became seriously ill with a bloodclot behind his right eye. He used music to heal himself. His book *The Mozart Effect* came out of his own experience with the transformational and healing powers of sound and music. He believes that we can use music to improve our memory and awareness, enhance our listening and attention-deficit disorders, heal mental disorders and physical injuries, activate creativity and reduce depression and anxiety.

When you listen to music, does it relax or energize you, or leave you feeling jangled? Be aware of how it affects your mood and health. Explore music as a healing and creative force in your life.

Mind over body

When I look into the future, it's so bright it burns my eyes.
Oprah Winfrey, talkshow host (b. 1954)

In a recent issue of the American journal *The Gerontologist*, Amy Lai, PhD, and her colleagues reported an important discovery. Their research concluded that people who were optimistic before heart surgery recovered more effectively than those who were not. They also discovered that those who engaged in private prayer were more optimistic on the day before surgery than those who did not.

Studies such as this one reconfirm the power of the mind to heal the body, and the power of prayer to uplift the mind. If you are having a health crisis or facing surgery, remember to focus on the positive. If possible, pray to God or a higher power for your illness to be healed.

Be your own life coach

There's only one corner of the universe you can be certain of improving, and that's your own self.
Aldous Huxley, author (1894–1963)

If you need help improving your life, you can hire a professional life coach. But, if you want to save money, consider coaching yourself.

First, see what's available on the Internet. Research careers as well as life-coaching techniques. Then check out the many new books available on self-coaching. By reading them, you'll help yourself clarify your goals, talents and interests. You'll also learn to motivate and encourage yourself on your chosen path. The books are wonderful, but don't forget to actively explore the career or activities you'd like to pursue. Do this by joining professional associations or support groups, and by attending meetings.

Use the serenity prayer

Serenity isn't freedom from the storm, but peace within the storm.

Anonymous

'God grant me the Serenity to accept the things I cannot change, Courage to change the things I can, and Wisdom to know the difference.' Theologian Reinhold Neibuhr wrote this prayer during the dark days of the Second World War, for presentation at a church service. And Bill W., founder of Alcoholics Anonymous, adapted it for use at AA meetings. Its power and simplicity remain relevant to us all.

Post this prayer on your refrigerator, and keep a copy on your desk at work. When life gets stressful, read or recite it. Think about the situation at hand. Perhaps you're having a problem at work – ask yourself if you have the power to change this situation for the better; or is it something over which you have no control and should therefore leave alone? Ask for wisdom to know the difference.

Have a stress-free wedding

All weddings, except those with shotguns in evidence, are wonderful.
Liz Smith, gossip columnist (b. 1923)

The social pressure to have a big, expensive wedding is hard to withstand. But a large, traditional wedding will cost you or your family enormous amounts of money.

If you want to keep it simple, insist on doing so. Make the celebration one that has meaning for you and your partner. Consider a more casual, fun and relaxed event without tuxedos and expensive dresses. Save money by hiring a standard photographer, not a wedding photographer. Buy your own alcohol and return whatever you don't use and get a refund. Rent a hall that's warm and friendly rather than regal and expensive. Get a local restaurant to provide the food. Hire student musicians, or get a friend to be a disc jockey and dance the night away.

Greet the soul

In the faces of men and women I see God.

Walt Whitman, poet (1819–92)

In India, when meeting someone you fold your hands at your heart, bow slightly and say '*Namaste*'. The greeting acknowledges the soul in the other person. The hands are folded at your 'heart chakra' (or energy centre) to tap into the flow of divine love.

The next time you greet someone, mentally fold your hands at your heart, and acknowledge their highest and deepest aspects. See if this changes the quality of your interaction and the way you think of them. When you are alone, practise *namaste* as a meditation to tap into your own soul and heart energy. Fold your hands at the heart level, bow your head and close your eyes. Imagine the divine filling your heart.

Accept change

Change is the law of life. And those who look only to the past or present are certain to miss the future.

John F. Kennedy, 35th president of the United States (1917–63)

If you find yourself dreading or avoiding change, you may be cheating yourself out of new and wonderful opportunities.

Are you afraid to take a great new job because it means moving to a new city? Are you scared to leave an unhealthy relationship because you're terrified to be alone? The nature of life is change, and nothing ever stays the same. Fear of change keeps you stranded on the river bank of life, when where you want to be is in the flow. If you're afraid of change in a particular situation, identify exactly what you're afraid of and list three actions you can take to alleviate your fears.

Act congruently

Happiness is when what you think, what you say and what you do are in harmony.

Mohandas K. Gandhi, political leader of India (1869–1948)

One of the best ways to simplify your life is to be 'on the same page' with yourself. In other words, your mind, your speech and your actions are congruent. This means that they 'come together' – they are in agreement, in harmony with one another.

When you find yourself thinking one thing and saying another, notice how you feel. An example would be agreeing with your patner to avoid conflict, when in fact you hold a different view. How does this affect you? If you think you shouldn't do something, but you do it anyway, do you end up feeling shame? Try to monitor yourself without judgement. Notice when you are not acting congruently. Work towards bringing what you think, say and do into harmony.

Bike to work

Every time I see an adult on a bicycle, I no longer despair for the future of the human race.

H. G. Wells, author (1866–1946)

Consider biking to work. Many cities provide bicycle paths and racks, and if you bike to work – even for part of the week – you'll enjoy better health, get some sunlight and fresh air, save on petrol, parking or public transportation, and relieve stress. You'll arrive at work feeling refreshed and energized for the day.

Be sure to invest in a safety helmet, and wear reflective gear if you ride home during the evening hours. Use a bicycle bag or panniers to carry your papers or work clothes. Check out bicycle clubs in your area. Getting together with other cyclists is a good way to find safer routes.

Think positive

*Our belief at the beginning of a doubtful undertaking is the one thing
that ensures the successful outcome of the venture.*
William James, psychologist (1842–1910)

Worry not only takes its toll on your health, but undermines all your
activities. Fear and doubt create outcomes in line with your thinking. In
other words, if you fear things won't work out successfully, then they
probably won't. On the other hand, if you cultivate a positive outlook,
your chances of enjoying positive outcomes increase.

List any current plans you may have – large or small, immediate or
long-term. Examine your thinking about these ventures. Write down any
negative thoughts or fears you may have. Counteract these pessimistic
thoughts by visualizing and writing down positive outcomes. Try to
practise positive thinking on a daily basis.

Make a difference

If you think you're too small to make a difference, you haven't been in bed with a mosquito.
Anita Roddick, entrepreneur and activist (b. 1942)

You may say, 'One person can't make a difference, so why bother?' But you *can* make a difference through volunteering. Once you open your heart to the idea, there will be no lack of opportunities.

Try teaching someone to read through a literacy programme, or working with a troubled teenager through your local school or church. And there are many organizations worldwide that care for homeless. Or if politics attracts you, dive in – work on an election, or work with a non-governmental organization. You'll make a difference for yourself and for others.

Rescue animals

The greatness of a nation can be judged by the way its animals are treated.

Mohandas K. Gandhi, political leader of India (1869–1948)

If you love animals, but don't have the money or lifestyle to keep a pet, consider volunteering for an animal rescue organization. Try looking on the Web or in your local phone book to locate one near you.

Some organizations rescue all types of animal, while others are animal- or breed-specific. Depending on what's available in your area, you may have the opportunity to care for birds, dogs, cats, horses, marsupials (if you live in Australia), deer, reptiles or farm animals (including pigs, goats and cows). If you do eventually want a pet of your own, working for a rescue organization can help you decide which one is right for you.

Learn to laugh at yourself

If I were given the opportunity to present a gift to the next generation, it would be the ability for each individual to learn to laugh at him or herself.
Charles Schulz, creator of the Peanuts comic strip (1922–2000)

It's easy to take yourself too seriously – to drown in shame if you make a mistake, and cling to an inflated or rigid view of yourself. Life is much easier if, once in a while, you step back and have a good laugh at your idiosyncrasies, your failures and your neurotic thinking and behaviour.

    If you're stressed out over your relationship, an overdue project or the massive dent you just put in your new car, take a minute, go for a walk and have a good laugh at your own expense. You'll relieve your stress, cut down on your perfectionism and have a much better perspective on life.

Plant trees

A man has made at least a start on discovering the meaning of human life when he plants shade trees under which he knows full well he will never sit.

D. Elton Trueblood, cartoonist (b. 1957)

You are not just a single individual, who lives and dies separate from the rest of nature and humanity. On the contrary, you are a citizen of the universe and are energetically connected to all other beings. As a citizen of the universe, and a resident of planet Earth, you are called to be a steward of her resources for those living in the present, and for future generations to come.

   Consider planting a tree every year, that others might enjoy them after you've gone. Thinking of your life in this connected, expanded and responsible way – and acting on that understanding – enhances your time here on Earth and, in time, may help you deepen your understanding of reality.

Limit violent images

We cannot continue polluting our minds.
Kalle Lasn, founder and editor of *Adbusters*

Television, movies and newspapers provide an overwhelming amount of violent imagery, 24 hours a day. Over time, this continuous bombardment of violent images has an unhealthy effect on your psyche. You end up with a very unbalanced view of life, and may become numb to what you are viewing or, worse, find yourself addicted to violence.

Consider how much violent imagery you're taking in on a daily basis. How is this affecting your mood and outlook on life? Consider not viewing any violent images for a week. Instead, consciously choose non-violent TV shows. This is not to deny that violence is a part of life. The purpose is to carefully monitor what you feed your mind.

Lie on the grass

To me a lush carpet of pine needles or spongy grass is more welcome than the most luxurious Persian rug.

Helen Keller, deaf-and-blind writer (1880–1968)

When was the last time you walked barefoot on grass, then flopped down spread-eagled, rolled over and enjoyed the warm sun? If the weather is suitable, find yourself a patch of lush grass and stretch out. Notice the soft feel and colour, the heady smells of the earth below, the warmth of the sun, the sound of insects buzzing and birds chirping. Let your body deeply relax. Breathe into any areas that are tense. Fall asleep if you want to.

Try doing this for 30 minutes a week, to ground you, relax you and renew your earth energy. When you're feeling unsupported, there's nothing better than letting Mother Earth hold you in her arms for a while.

Save on energy bills

Being frugal, one has abundance.

Lao-tsu, author of the *Tao Te Ching* (6th century BCE)

Reduce your heating and cooling needs to save money, and help the environment at the same time. Start by upgrading the insulation in your ceiling, walls and other areas, as needed. Replace old windows. Caulk any holes and cracks to prevent energy loss. Install programmable thermostats, and turn down the heat at night. Be sure to maintain your boiler and air-conditioning and, if you're able to, buy an energy-efficient washing machine, spin dryer and refrigerator.

Obviously, before you can realize long-term savings, you may have to spend money in the short term. Research the best prices on what you'll need. Set aside funds in a bank account, on a monthly basis, until you reach your target amount.

Examine your motivation

The quality of your actions depends on your motivation.

Gehlek Rimpoche, lama (b. 1939)

What you do in life matters. However, your motivation matters more. The same action could be positive or negative, depending on your reasons for doing it.

For the next week, review the motivation for all your actions. Are you motivated by your own fame or gain, or are you motivated to benefit others as well? Do you work simply for a pay cheque, or do you work to make a positive difference in the world? Experiment with changing your motivation and see if it alters how you feel about what you do. The idea is not to judge yourself. Try to have a larger, more inclusive motivation for everything you do, in order to enhance the quality of your life.

Use non-toxic home products

Natural alternatives are nourishing and life-giving, a stark contrast to those dead chemicals that line our shelves.

Annie Berthold-Bond, author of *Better Basics for the Home*

Present-day cleaning products remove grease and dirt, but they contain skin irritants and introduce toxic chemicals and fumes into your environment. Commercial indoor pesticides are especially dangerous and should be avoided.

In order to save your health, switch to non-toxic, fragrance-free cleaners. Look on the packaging for words like 'biodegradable', 'unscented', 'uncoloured' and 'environmentally friendly'. Identify brands that use natural ingredients. You can usually find these on sale at health-food stores.

If you want to save money, make your own cleaning products from simple ingredients such as lemon, vinegar, baking soda, washing soda and coconut oil. For pest control, use natural products such as borax, or electronic, ultrasonic devices.

Learn from your demons

Every part of our personality that we do not love will become hostile to us.
Robert Bly, author and poet (b. 1926)

Do your destructive aspects cause you to suffer? Do you smoke too much or over-eat? Do you have a bad temper? Are you irresponsible with money?

Consider your destructive aspects as your demons. You may deny that you have demons altogether; or, if you admit you have them, you may judge yourself harshly. A better way to work with your demons is to love them. For instance, if you smoke, visualize your smoking demon as a thin, ill, tobacco-stained man. Ask him what you can do to make him feel better. He may reveal that he is afraid and anxious about work and money. By being compassionate with your demons, you lessen their mischief. Learn from them how to give up your negative behaviour and take care of your unmet needs.

Improve your sleep

What we need to do is create bedrooms that are very serene, restful and very good at getting us to relax.

Terah Kathryn Collins, author of *The Western School Guide to Feng Shui*

The ancient Chinese art of feng shui is dedicated to enhancing the environment and energy around you. If you're having trouble sleeping, consider the following feng shui advice.

First, remove the TV, computer and any exercise equipment from your bedroom, to make the room as serene as possible. If your bed is opposite a mirror, cover the mirror with a cloth at night. Position your bed so that you can see the door, but are not directly in front of it. Try not to sleep next to a window. Place your bed against a wall or use a solid headboard. Make sure there is nothing hanging directly overhead, such as a light fixture, a ceiling fan or a beam.

Cultivate compassion

Relieving someone of any problem, even a simple headache, with the motivation of compassion, has tremendous benefit.
Gehlek Rimpoche, lama (b. 1939)

You may think that cultivating compassion is something you do for someone else. But when you generate compassion for others you do it for yourself as well. Regardless of the effect of your thoughts or actions on others, it's you who will feel the greatest happiness and contentment.

When you find yourself in a difficult or stressful situation with someone, regardless of how you feel about them, generate the wish to relieve his or her suffering. By doing this you take your focus off your own distress, and you lessen your own anger or anxiety. As you open your heart to him or her, you make it possible to resolve your differences. The key to your own happiness is cultivating compassion for others.

Practise aural self-acupressure

The ear is considered by acupuncturists one of the most important parts of the body.

Wataru Ohashi, author of *Do-It-Yourself Shiatsu*

There are many ways to enhance your health through self-acupressure massage. According to traditional Japanese medicine, our ears reflect our entire body. Imagine the ear as an inverted foetus, with the earlobe as the head. Each ear contains about 200 acupressure points that correspond to all areas of our body. By massaging various points on your ears, you can relieve anxiety, help addictions, ease pain and promote weight loss.

You don't have to know where each point is in order to obtain benefits. Once daily, to relax and energize yourself, gently pull and stretch your earlobes and ears away from your head. Then use your fingertips to massage every surface of your ear, inside and out. To learn about specific points, consult a guide on acupressure or shiatsu.

Be a visionary

*Dive into the labyrinth, risk getting lost, and return to your own
community with bright ideas that help people see themselves and the
world differently.*

Eric Utne, founder of *Utne Reader* magazine

Be a visionary for your own life. Identify five people whom you think of
as visionaries. Ask yourself what makes them so. Are they original
thinkers in their field? Are they especially creative or gifted? Do they
contribute to a better world for everyone?

Now, imagine you're having dinner with one of the visionaries you've
identified. Tell them about your past life, and about your hopes and
dreams for the future. Ask for their help in envisioning your life in a fresh,
new way. Discuss with them how you can achieve your vision. Ask them
to be your mentor. If they agree, call on them for advice whenever you
feel you need it.

Make lemonade out of life's lemons

One who can find lemons sweet and grapes sour is ready for Dame Fortune.

Mason Cooley, aphorist (b. 1927)

Life is full of difficulties. If things are going well, just wait! Like the weather, things often change. One day you're wealthy, then the stock market crashes and you lose everything. You go into work on a Friday afternoon, and by 3 p.m. you're packing your belongings, dismissal notice in hand. You're in perfect health today, and tomorrow you're diagnosed with cancer.

Tragedies make you to want give up on life. But look closely – there's opportunity hidden in those ashes. If misfortune befalls you, grieve for your loss. Ask yourself how can you make the best of it. Express gratitude to God and the universe for giving you the chance to start anew. Then make lemonade out of the lemons life has given you.

Love the body you have

What you need is an acceptance of yourself as you are.

Chungliang Al Huang, author of *Embrace Tiger, Return to Mountain*

One of the keys to a simpler life is accepting yourself as you are. Reduce your stress and anxiety by the simple act of loving yourself. Because social pressures to be thin are rampant, it's especially important to love the body you have.

First of all, don't put yourself down. Comparing yourself to movie stars is self-torture. Concentrate on how your body feels, rather than how it looks. Be active: walk, run, do yoga, dance. List your assets and positive qualities. Do you have a good sense of humour? Are you kind? Are you a loving partner or parent? Look into the mirror and love the person looking back at you. Concentrate on living your life to the full.

Give kids what they really need

A child's ability to cope and thrive lies in that child's having had at least a small, safe place (an apartment? a room? a lap?) in which, in the companionship of a loving person, that child could discover that he or she was lovable and capable of loving in return.

Fred Rogers, TV personality and author (1928–2003)

Your children may be demanding this new toy or that expensive pair of trainers because they are learning from you, and from TV advertising, that 'things' are a priority. They are needy, you are exhausted, no one is happy and no one feels appreciated.

Bottom line: your children want to feel loved and respected. They want your wisdom and guidance. They want affection, safety and boundaries. They want your approval. They want your time. If your life is such that you aren't giving your kids what money can't buy, reconsider your priorities. Find a way to give them what they really need.

Walk, don't ride

*Restore human legs as a means of travel. Pedestrians rely on food for
fuel and need no special parking facilities.*

Lewis Mumford, author and humanist (1895–1990)

One of the reasons why obesity is on the rise is because we don't walk
as much as we ride. It's easy to jump in your car, drive that half mile and
be there instantly. On the other hand, walking half a mile would take you
about ten minutes. You'd be much healthier, less stressed and over time
you'd probably lose some weight.

Traffic congestion is also on the rise. If you drove less, you'd help cut
down on congestion, parking lots and pollution. Over time, try to
gradually increase your walking and decrease your driving and riding.

Keep your mind sharp

The whole business of marshalling one's energies becomes more and more important as one grows older.

Hume Cronyn, actor and screenwriter (1911–2003)

As you age it's important to maintain your health. You may already work out, eat well and get regular check-ups, but you may not have considered doing anything to maintain your mind. As you grow older your mental sharpness decreases. With some effort, you can offset this natural decline. Try the following suggestions.

Increase your mind power by taking ginkgo, a herb known to improve concentration, boost memory, alleviate depression and help patients in the early stages of Alzheimer's. Be sure to exercise your mind as well as your body – this keeps your brain oxygenated and balances your hormones. Learn something new. Taking on a new subject, or learning a new activity, keeps you young by creating fresh pathways in your brain.

Take a volunteer holiday

Never doubt that a small group of thoughtful citizens can change the world. Indeed, it is the only thing that ever has.
Margaret Mead, anthropologist (1901–78)

Many volunteer organizations around the globe provide opportunities for individuals, families or groups to spend their holiday volunteering their services to help others. Activities range from working on archaeological digs to restoring trails in national parks and counting wildlife. Most volunteer holidays cost less than going to the same location as a tourist and provide a more enriching experience. Service holidays are first and foremost about service, yet you'll always have some free time in which to explore on your own.

Search for 'service vacations' or 'international volunteerism' on the Internet to find an organization offering a programme right for you.

Don't practise 'spaving'

The safest way to double your money is to fold it over and put it in your pocket.

Kin Hubbard, American cartoonist (1868–1930)

When you want something that costs a certain amount, and it suddenly goes on sale for half price, you rush to buy it, rejoicing that you just *saved* half the cost. You might even buy two and save the full amount! But the reality is that you just spent the half price or full amount – you didn't *save* anything.

'Spave' is a newly coined word that means 'to spend money on items priced below normal retail cost, and therefore save the difference'. The word obviously confuses 'reducing spending' with the actual practice of 'accumulating money'. Spaving may be one reason for your growing credit-card debt and your shrinking or non-existent savings account. Whether you're shopping at a mall, on a home TV network or on the Internet, the next time you find yourself wanting to *spave*, try saving instead.

Make time to worry

Leave your worry on the doorstep.
Dorothy Fields, songwriter of 'On the Sunny Side of the Street'

If you're human, you worry. What you worry about is unique to you. Instead of worrying as problems arise, try setting aside a regular time to worry.

Find a notebook, a pen and a serene spot where you won't be disturbed. List everything you're worried about. Prioritize your worries according to what stresses you the most. Then brainstorm solutions for each worry. For instance, if you're worried about a health problem, write down three things you might do to help yourself. If you're worried about your deteriorating relationship with your partner, write down three actions you might take to strengthen your relationship.

Be sure to stick to whatever schedule you've set for worrying, and limit your worrying at other times. By doing this you'll have much more control over your life and your problems.

Stop mowing your lawn

*If I rounded up everybody I know who enjoys landscape maintenance,
they would fit comfortably into the back seat of a Yugo.*
Andy Wasowski, author of *Landscaping Revolution*

Lawnmowers that run on petrol are noisy and fill the air with pollution.
Mowing a lawn takes up precious time, which is always better spent
doing something else. One solution is to get rid of your lawn altogether.

Instead of having a lawn, plant native shrubs, wild flowers,
vegetables and trees. Add a rock garden, stone paths and garden
benches for relaxing on. Besides being beautiful, native plants are
invaluable to wildlife, providing berries and seeds for birds, while small
mammals rely on them for shelter. If you want to reserve a patch of
grass for the kids to play on, keep it small and mow it with an old-
fashioned, hand-powered, push mower.

Live in shared housing

We are a group of people dedicated to creating a place where resources are shared, lives are simplified, the Earth is respected, diversity is welcomed, children play together in safety, and living in community with neighbours comes naturally.

Sunward Co-Housing, an intentional community in Ann Arbor, Michigan

Shared-housing communities combine traditional home ownership with shared common facilities and ongoing relationships with your neighbours. Their purpose is to counteract the alienation of modern housing, where no one knows their neighbour and there's no sense of community. The communities of 20 or 30 families are usually designed and managed by the residents. Most include a broad mix of ages, and both singles and family groups.

If you want to live more simply, and in community with others, check on the Internet for shared-housing communities near you. Most allow visitors by appointment. If you want to see if this lifestyle is for you, try joining a community by renting a place for six months.

Heal yourself with laughter

If taking vitamins doesn't keep you healthy enough, try more laughter: The most wasted of all days is that on which one has not laughed.
Nicolas-Sébastien Chamfort, writer (1741–94)

When you laugh, you lower your blood pressure, reduce your stress and increase the oxygen levels in your blood, making you feel more energized. You also increase your endorphin levels, which makes you feel great. Laughter even gives your muscles a workout.

If you're feeling down and you want to laugh, you have to make an effort. Watch a movie that you know makes you laugh, read the cartoons in the newspaper, watch a TV sitcom or sign up for a free joke service on the Internet. If you're upset about the state of the world, read some political satire. And when you read the morning paper don't skip the funnies. When it comes to your health, laughter is a serious business!

Be enthusiastic

Every great and commanding moment in the annals of the world is the triumph of some enthusiasm.

Ralph Waldo Emerson, author and poet (1803–82)

The word 'enthusiasm' comes from the Greek word *entheos*, meaning 'to be inspired by a god'. The magic power of enthusiasm is within all of us, waiting to empower our endeavours, improve our relationships and encourage others on their path. It's the fuel that gets things done. It's the contagious energy that inspires.

If you're having trouble achieving what you want, or are feeling somewhat lazy and unmotivated, consider meditating on the power of enthusiasm. Imagine what it would be to feel 'inspired by a god' in all that you do. Engage yourself in pursuing your highest purpose and look for spiritual inspiration to guide you. Your enthusiasm can help focus and motivate you, and others, towards positive goals.

Take a five-minute break

No matter how much pressure you feel at work, if you could find ways to relax for at least five minutes every hour, you'd be more productive.
Dr Joyce Brothers, psychologist and author (b. 1949)

You may work for three or four hours at your computer without getting up. When you finally stop, you're exhausted. Your body is cramped, your shoulders are slumped, your eyes are burning and your breathing is shallow. Yet, although you may be working long hours, you may not be as productive as you think.

Take five minutes out of every hour to stand up and stretch. Then gently palm your eyes and rub your temples. Take a few deep breaths, and if possible take a short walk. You'll be much more productive, and healthier both physically and mentally, at the end of the day.

Pay attention

Life is denied by lack of attention, whether it be to cleaning windows or trying to write a masterpiece.

Nadia Boulanger, musical composition teacher (1887–1979)

Bringing your full attention to bear on whatever you're doing is essential to all accomplishments, however lofty or mundane. It's a skill that takes practice, and it's developed with effort. Many self-help books recommend multi-tasking – reading while you eat, watching TV while you cook, reading and answering emails while talking on the phone. However, no one wrote a symphony while making dinner.

Breathe deeply for a few moments before you begin a task. Let go of all thoughts, except those that pertain to what you are about to do. Bring all your intention to focus on the work before you. Notice whether you feel more interested in life when you practise single-minded attention on the task in hand.

Become a freelance air courier

Travel by its very nature demands simplicity. If you don't believe this, just go home and try stuffing everything you own into a backpack.
Rolf Potts, author of *Vagabonding*

If you want to travel to many exciting cities around the world for a fraction of the cost, try becoming a freelance air courier. Freelance couriers accompany cargo on a commercial airline for a courier company. The cargo is shipped as your luggage, and may be anything from documents to equipment. You don't handle the cargo, but upon arrival you're responsible for delivering the 'manifest' or paperwork to the customs officials. In exchange for your service, the company gives you a reduced-rate, economy, round-trip airline ticket. Savings can range from 25 to 50 per cent, and your return is within a one- to two-week period. Courier opportunities have diminished somewhat since 9/11, but they're still worth checking out.

Risk being who you are

Death is not the biggest fear we have; our biggest fear is taking the risk to be alive – the risk to be alive and express what we really are.
Don Miguel Ruiz, author of *The Four Agreements*

Social and family pressures sometimes cause us to suppress and deny our true natures. You may be in a profession that is socially acceptable and pleases your family, but has nothing to do with what you *really* want to do.

Are you a lawyer who wants to write novels, a nurse who wants to be a doctor, or an accountant who wants to work with animals? Are you in a relationship that isn't working? Do you want to explore another religion? The important thing is to risk expressing what you're not articulating in your life, because not to do so means you are denying yourself the joy of authentic living.

Create your own ceremonies

When humans participate in ceremony, they enter a sacred space. Emotions flow more freely ... All is made new; everything becomes sacred.

Sun Bear, Native American chief (b. 1929)

We have modern-day celebrations such as birthday parties, weddings, graduations and festivals of all kinds. But we have lost the power of ritual and ceremony – practices that mark and elevate our transitions in life, that honour the seasons, that begin new ventures.

Consider creating your own rituals or ceremonies for yourself, and for your friends and loved ones. Start by creating a ceremony for the next transition in your life. If you have a new job, create a ritual with your partner or a friend, using symbolic objects, flowers, candles, incense and clothing. Express your intention for this new work to be spiritually, emotionally and financially rewarding.

Dematerialize

You can never get enough of what you don't need to make you happy.
Eric Hoffer, docker and author (1902–83)

When you see something you want, you get excited. You research your potential purchase, and weigh up the pros and cons of different models. You think about having it, and a warm glow temporarily fills your body. You know that having this item will make you happy. You imagine it will make you feel sexy, cause you to be more attractive or simply give you great pleasure and happiness from owning it. You comparison-shop locally and online. Finally you make your decision. You buy it, and bring it home. It's great! For 24–48 hours, you're in heaven. A week later the item is starting to fade from your consciousness. A month later you have forgotten about it. You've moved on to the next item.

Material possessions can bring you temporary pleasure, but they don't lead to happiness.

Start a reading group

Go three days without reading and your speech will become tasteless.
Chinese proverb

If you love to read, a great way to share your passion for reading is to start a reading group. Reading groups, or book clubs, are great ways to stay connected with friends, meet new friends and participate in your community.

Organize your reading group or book club according to genre (such as fiction or poetry) or subject matter (such as current events or spirituality). If you meet in members' homes, combine your meetings with pot-luck meals or dessert and coffee. If your group is larger, try reserving a room at your local church or library. Some book shops are happy to provide meeting space. To help build a strong group, keep the meeting time consistent and limit your discussion time to two hours.

Embrace the mysterious

The most beautiful thing we can experience is the mysterious. He to whom this emotion is a stranger, who can no longer pause to wonder and stand rapt in awe, is as good as dead.
Albert Einstein, theoretical physicist (1879–1955)

The mysterious attracts and pulls us like a magnet, yet its meaning eludes us. Mystery takes us out of our literal mind and into a world larger than ourselves. The mysterious delights, frightens, stimulates, engenders awe and opens our hearts.

Do you prefer to stick to the literal and the known, or do you let yourself ponder the mysteries of life. Do you wonder how far the universe extends? Or how we came into being? Do you think about life after death, one of the biggest mysteries of all? When you feel life is too small and predictable, remember that life is full of mystery.

Make every act count

*I want to convince you that you must learn to make every act count,
since you are going to be here only for a short while, in fact, too short
for witnessing all the marvels of it.*

Don Juan, shaman, quoted by author Carlos Castaneda

Contemplate the shortness of your life and find a renewed appreciation
of the importance of every moment. With that appreciation, make better
choices and more conscious decisions about how you spend your time.

Everything you do is important. Make every act count by making sure
that your actions are life-enhancing for yourself and others, and in line
with your highest values and deepest spiritual intent. Stop doing things
that don't fit with who you are and what you want to be. At the end of
your day, look over what you did from this perspective: what actions
were best left undone, and which actions contributed to your life?

Be flexible

Better to bend than to break.
French proverb

Flexibility of body, mind and spirit is equally important. How flexible are you physically? Can you touch your toes? How flexible are you in your thinking? Do you always have to be right, or are you open to learning something new? How flexible are you in spirit? Are you willing to take life as it comes, and adjust when necessary?

For greater flexibility in your body, explore yoga. For flexibility in your thinking, take a class and engage in dialogue with your teacher and fellow students, with the intention of learning something. For flexibility of spirit, monitor any rigidity in your approach to life. When you feel resistance to what life presents, relax your body and imagine yourself as a willow tree. Be rooted, yet flexible.

Make clear choices

What we have to contribute is both unique and irreplaceable. What we withhold from life is lost from life. The entire world depends upon our individual choices.

Duane Elgin, author of *Voluntary Simplicity*

Think of your life as a series of choices. For every past action, you made a choice, whether or not you were conscious of making one. You may reflect on a past situation and say, 'I had no choice, I had to do it.' However, no matter how trapped you may have felt, you made a choice.

You make choices hundreds of times a day, from the inconsequential to the profound. Knowing that you're choosing all your actions brings clarity, responsibility and accountability to your life. Each evening, ask yourself if your choices that day have contributed positively to your life and to the universe.

See God everywhere

*The kingdom will not come by expectation. The kingdom of the father is
spread over the earth and men do not see it.*

The Gospel according to St Thomas

Where is God? Where is Buddha, Yahweh, Christ or Krishna? Does your
God or higher power reside somewhere else, other than in this world?
However you experience 'God', at times he or she can seem remote,
especially when you are undergoing difficulties.

Imagine that God is everywhere: beside you at breakfast,
in the grove of pine trees down the road, in the flowers
growing in your garden, in the people you love and in
the air you breathe. Imagine God sustaining you
through your joy and suffering. Imagine God near
you and around you at all times.

How does the notion of God 'spread over
the earth' change the way you think of God?

Love your work

Choose a job you love, and you will never have to work a day in your life.
Confucius, philosopher (551–479 BC)

If you have a job you hate, you may not believe it's possible to love work. But hating your work takes its toll on your health and well-being. Because work takes up so much of your life energy, it's important to love what you do.

If jobs are scarce, you may need to stay where you are. But you can help yourself by changing your attitude towards work. Find whatever positives you can in your current job and focus on them. Use your free time to explore what you really want to do. Get active. Enroll in classes. Hire a life coach. Talk to people who do what you'd like to do. Prepare yourself to manifest the work you love.

Create your future

My future is in my past and my past is my present. I must now make the present my future.

Vladimir Horowitz, pianist (1904–89)

The tarot, runes and astrology are all forms of divination that we can use to predict our futures. They are based on the notion that energy forces are at play in the universe that, if allowed to unfold, can lead to certain outcomes. These energies are, however, not fate. You, as an actor in your life, can shape your future by working with or against these energetic forces.

So, if you really want to predict your future, begin now to imagine it. Don't wait passively for it to unfold. What do you want to happen – next week, next month or next year? Keep asking these questions, and start creating your future the way you want it to be.

Act boldly

Whatever you can do, or dream you can – begin it. Boldness has genius, power and magic in it.

Johann Wolfgang von Goethe, poet and dramatist (1749–1832)

If you have a dream of something you'd like to do, don't leave it buried in the pages of your journal or perpetually on the 'back burner' of your mind. You may think your dreams are out of reach, but you *can* make them a reality simply by taking the first step.

If you want to quit your job and find another, start reading the job ads. If you want to get married, start by asking someone out on a date. If you want to own a house, go and look at houses for sale. Your dream may seem distant, but the act of beginning – even with one small step – will energize you. That energy 'magic' and 'boldness' generated by taking the first step will carry you forward towards realizing your dreams.

Cure your despair

Action is the antidote to despair.
Joan Baez, folk singer (b. 1941)

If you're in despair over the violence in the world, the fact that children go to bed hungry, the high cost of health care, the spread of AIDS, global warming, corporate corruption or other problems specific to your own community, the best cure is to take some action to remedy the wrongs. Any action (however small or insignificant) contributes to positive change and lifts you from your sense of hopelessness.

Write a letter to your local newspaper, work for a politician who can make a difference, join a social-change organization dealing with the problems that concern you, or volunteer your time to give direct aid to those in need.

Grow roots

To be rooted is perhaps the most important and least recognized need of the human soul.

Simone Weil, philosopher (1909–43)

We move a great deal in the 21st century. Maybe you've packed your bags and moved to another city for a better job, or even to another country. Or maybe you still live in the town of your birth. No matter where you live, it's important to feel rooted and to have the feeling of being at home.

Your real roots are your internal supports: your values, your emotions, your aspirations and your spiritual path. Grow your internal roots by knowing who you are, what you believe and what you want to accomplish in life.

Visualize your roots, then draw them on paper. Label each root and describe how it supports you.

Stay curious

Never lose a holy curiosity.
Albert Einstein, theoretical physicist (1879–1955)

You are born curious, with an open and questioning mind. But your enthusiasm may get squelched, at school and at work, where everyone seems to want answers instead of questions. It's time to reclaim the purity and innocence of your 'holy curiosity'. In a notebook, make a list of 50 questions that are important to you. Don't hesitate to sound naive. Ask 'Why is the sky blue?' if you want to. Pursue the answers to your questions.

Next, make a list of 50 things you would like to learn, if you had the opportunity. Do you want to try yoga, or become a firefighter? Write it down. Then choose one new skill and take a class. If you keep your curiosity alive, your life will be endlessly interesting.

Forgive

It is the act of forgiveness that opens up the only possible way to think creatively about the future at all.

Father Desmond Wilson, Catholic priest and activist (b. 1925)

If you forgive, you may feel you have to swallow your pain or be vulnerable to further harm. But you can express your feelings, set healthy boundaries *and* forgive, regardless of what the other person feels, says or does.

Recall times when you have hurt others and have been glad of their forgiveness. Recognize that no one is perfect. If you know the person who has hurt you, forgive them, even if you end your relationship. If the person is a stranger, forgive them regardless of what they did. Not forgiving kills your compassion and keeps you frozen in the past. Forgiveness of others, and yourself, is essential if you are to move freely into your future.

Have self-respect

Never violate the sacredness of your individual self-respect.
Theodore Parker, theologian, pastor and scholar (1810–60)

When you look in the mirror, do you have respect for the person staring back at you? Are you living your life with dignity, in line with the values you want to uphold? If you can't answer 'Yes', ask yourself why not. What would you have to do to regain your self-respect?

Perhaps you're doing work that pays well, but ultimately harms other people. If so, try to find more positive employment. If you're in a relationship that is demeaning, leave it. If you have an addiction, get help. If you harmed someone, make amends. Self-respect takes self-love, self-compassion and ongoing maintenance.

Decide how you're going to live

You don't get to choose how you're going to die. Or when. You can only decide how you're going to live. Now.

Joan Baez, folk singer (b. 1941)

At least once a year ask yourself if you're living the life you want to be living. Have you made clear and conscious decisions about your friends and lovers, your work, what kind of house you live in, what part of the world you call home, and what spiritual path you've chosen?

Ask yourself what you would do if you could do anything your heart desired. If you've simply never thought about what you *really* want, write down what your ideal life would look like. Describe a typical day. Where would you be living, who would be with you, what work would you be doing? Then take steps to start living the life you want. Now.

Be open to difference

Some of the most wonderful people are the ones who don't fit into boxes.

Tori Amos, musician (b. 1963)

We humans are social animals. We like to sort ourselves into 'types', with neat labels such as 'intellectual', 'housewife' or 'professional'. When we can't place someone neatly in a category, we may feel uneasy around them. We might say, 'I don't know what to make of them.'

The truth is that no one comfortably wears any social label. Even those of us who appear to fit neatly in social 'boxes' are as complex and unique as snowflakes. So don't avoid people whom you can't fit into a pigeonhole. Accept them for their unique and special qualities.

Make enjoyment your wealth

Not what we have, but what we enjoy, constitutes our abundance.
Epicurus, philosopher (341–271 BCE)

Epicurus taught that enjoyment was a mental activity. According to this ancient Greek philosopher, your mind and your attitude towards life – rather than the acquisition of material possessions – represent your sole source of pleasure.

Are you capable of enjoying life in the moment, regardless of what you have or don't have? If you're sipping a cup of coffee right now, savour it. If the sun is setting, take the time to enjoy the display. If you love your new car, enjoy driving it, but know that the car itself isn't making you happy – you are. Enjoyment comes from inside. It's an approach to life that requires a light touch, the ability to bask in the sensual and the capacity to let go. It doesn't require money. Your ability to enjoy life is your wealth.

Have compassion
for all beings

Compassion, in which all ethics must take root, can only attain its full breadth and depth if it embraces all living creatures and does not limit itself to mankind.
Albert Schweitzer, theologian, physician and missionary (1875–1965)

Just like you, all beings want to be happy and avoid suffering – even the little ant that scurries across your floor, the birds that leave their calling card on your car, the rabbits that eat your garden, the colleague who annoys you, and your partner who squeezes the toothpaste tube in the wrong place.

Practising compassion for all living creatures – no matter how difficult it may be – transforms your life. It turns your aggression into peace, and your anger into patience and understanding. It changes your self-hate into self-love.

Move to a smaller city

A great city is not to be confounded with a populous one.
Aristotle, philosopher (384–322 BCE)

People often gravitate to big cities because there's more opportunity for work, more excitement, more shops, more of everything. However, if your goal is to simplify your life, consider living in a smaller city or town. The advantages often outweigh the lack of big-city excitement. You'll enjoy a lower cost of living, an easier pace of life, less crime and usually more friendliness.

You may be worried about supporting yourself in a smaller city. However, you'll be able to get by on a smaller income in a less populous area. If you decide you want to move, take your time and do your research. Look for resources on the comparative cost of living and the quality of life in various cities around the world.

Live in the now

No valid plans for the future can be made by those who have no capacity for living now.

Alan W. Watts, philosopher (1915–73)

Try sitting quietly for a few moments. Notice what thoughts appear. If you're like most mortals, you'll find yourself thinking of past events, or speculating about the future. It's difficult to be totally present and focused in the moment. But if you never dwell fully in the present your future will simply be a continuation of not living in the present. Only by making an effort to be in the present moment can you reliably know who you are and what you want.

Do this by using your senses. Take in what is around you, and notice how you feel. Make a practice of living in the now. Then use the insights you gain to plan your future. In this way your future will serve you well.

Expose prejudice

Prejudice is like a hair across your cheek. You can't see it, you can't find it with your fingers, but you keep brushing at it because the feel of it is irritating.

Marian Anderson, singer (1902–93)

If you're prejudiced in any way, you judge people before getting to know them. When you meet someone for the first time, do you let their race, dress, age, gender or appearance cause you to make conclusions about their character, intelligence, trustworthiness or abilities?

Because of past experiences or social training, you may have conscious or unconscious prejudices. When you meet someone new, ask yourself if you have any preconceived ideas about this person for any reason. Try to set those prejudices aside, and be open to them as another human being worthy of your respect. Don't let your prejudices keep you from life.

Live within your means

Bring your desires down to your present means. Increase them only when your increased means permit.

Aristotle, philosopher (384–322 BCE)

In the 4th century BCE, Aristotle obviously didn't know about advertising and credit cards, the two main reasons why personal debt is on the rise. He suggested reducing your desires to fit your present means – easy for him to say! Our culture encourages desires of every kind, 24 hours a day, seven days a week, because encouraging desire sells things.

Yet Aristotle's advice is still sound, even in a world where it's hard to not want things and not over-spend. For one month, avoid all advertising as much as possible. Enjoy – and rejoice in – the possessions you already have. Spend less than you take in and put some money in your savings account. Feeling financially grounded and in control offsets the stress of living beyond your means.

Look at the sky

The sky is the daily bread of the eyes.
Ralph Waldo Emerson, author and poet (1803–82)

If you live in the country, you probably look at the sky every day. If you live in a city, you probably don't. Yet, if you're forgetting to look skyward, you're missing one of the glories of the universe.

The sky is exquisitely beautiful, its changeableness infinite, its colours breathtaking. Its clouds take on the shapes of birds, rabbits and menacing dragons, or envelop everything in a beautiful mist. They have great Latin names such as cumulus, stratus, cirrus and nimbus.

Give your mind a rest, and your soul some inspiration, by looking at the sky above for five minutes a day.

Live with open hands

We enter the world with closed hands, as if to say, 'The world is mine.' We leave it with open hands, as if to say, 'Behold, I take nothing with me.'

from The Midrash, a Jewish commentary on biblical texts (400–500 CE)

The phrase 'You can't take it with you' is probably as old as humankind. Yet, knowing that, we still cling to our money and possessions. We even write wills and trusts, planning to manage them from the grave.

Close your eyes and imagine that you own nothing. Imagine you're simply a steward of your possessions while you're alive. The day you die, they revert to the universe. If you think of your possessions in this way, it helps to loosen your grip on them, and lessen your anxiety about what you have or don't have. Rather than clinging to your possessions, live with open hands and an open heart.

Be the change

You must be the change you wish to see in the world.

Mohandas K. Gandhi, political leader of India (1869–1948)

If you want world peace, the next time you want to yell at someone, don't. If you want the world to be less materialistic, don't shop as entertainment. If you want to eradicate terrorism, stem your own anger and hatred. If you want to feed the hungry, be more mindful of what you eat. If you want the world to be more spiritual, give more time to your spiritual practice. If you want more equality in the world, treat everyone equally. By changing yourself, you'll feel less powerless. By changing yourself, you change the world.

Grow flowers

The earth laughs in flowers.

Ralph Waldo Emerson, author and poet (1803–82)

Flowers have deep roots in the human psyche. We use flowers to mark our special events, such as births, weddings or funerals. We take them to friends in hospital. We give them to lovers. We grace our homes and our tables with them. We wear them in our hair and pin them on our clothes.

Get a seed catalogue and decide which flowers you love most. Then buy seeds or seedlings and plant them in your garden, on a balcony or in a windowbox. Consider both colour and scent. Grow roses, tulips and daffodils and the stately iris. Plant bulbs, flowering trees and bushes. Let flowers make your world more beautiful and fragrant. Enjoy sharing them with others.

Believe in your recovery

Drugs are not always necessary, but belief in recovery always is.
Norman Cousins, author and essayist (1912–90)

Whether you have a simple cold or something more serious, such as heart disease or cancer, belief in your recovery is your best ally.

Close your eyes and visualize your illness in whatever form seems right to you. For example, you might see it as small green cells spread throughout your body. Imagine sitting in a beautiful tropical location, under a warm waterfall. Ask God or your higher power to assist you in removing your illness. See the water pouring over and through your body. Visualize your illness being washed through your body and leaving through your toes. Regardless of how you actually feel, think of yourself as completely healed and full of energy. Believe in your recovery.

Appreciate the basic necessities

Like when I'm in the bathroom looking at my toilet paper, I'm like 'Wow! That's toilet paper?' I don't know if we appreciate how much we have.
Alicia Silverstone, actress (b. 1976)

When you hit the light switch, do you appreciate the light that illuminates your room? When you turn on the tap and water flows, do you marvel at having running water? When you pick up your telephone and dial a number, do you feel the magic when someone next door – or around the world – says hello?

Set aside a few minutes each day to appreciate the basics that you take for granted – from the toilet paper to the silverware and the shoes on your feet. This deep appreciation of the simple necessities of life keeps your awareness keen, brings tremendous joy and ensures that you'll never take anything for granted.

Keep your heart unwrinkled

To keep the heart unwrinkled, to be hopeful, kindly, cheerful, reverent, is to triumph over old age.
Thomas B. Aldrich, author (1836–1907)

It's inevitable – some day you're going to have wrinkles; if not now, then at some time in the future. When the inevitable happens, and your youth begins to fade, don't waste your money on expensive creams, hair colouring or plastic surgery. If you want a real antidote to ageing, keep your heart young.

No matter what's happening in your life, or in the world, have hope that tomorrow will be better. Practise optimism in the face of any personal disasters. Don't focus on your aches and pains. Stay cheerful regardless of how you feel. Be kind to yourself and those around you. Bow in reverence, on a daily basis, to the beauty and mystery of your precious life.

Have a beginner's mind

If you actually learn to like being a beginner, the whole world opens up to you.

Barbara Sher, author of *I Could Do Anything If I Only Knew What It Was*

Buddhist teachers encourage their students to have a 'beginner's mind'. The idea is that if you keep your mind free of incessant thought and preconceived notions, there's no limit to what you can experience and learn. In fact, you can become enlightened!

On the other hand, if you like to be in control, have the right answers, be on top of your game and always have the last word, you're cheating yourself. All that energy you expend on being an expert wears you out and keeps you from the joy of learning.

Regardless of your accumulated knowledge and expertise, become a lifelong beginner. Learn to listen to others, allow yourself to be moved and be willing to change your thinking. Strive to learn something new every day.

Heal your wounds

A wounded deer leaps the highest.
Emily Dickinson, poet (1830–86)

If you're human, you probably suffered some kind of emotional or physical wounding in your childhood or later in life. Maybe you were abused in some way, or your partner left you, or you suffered a serious accident. You can try to deny your wounds and distance yourself from painful memories, or you can get help and heal yourself.

Heal your pain, and watch your wounds turn into your best assets. They can transform into wisdom and knowledge, and deepen your sensitivity and compassion for yourself and others. If you want to, you can be of great help to those who have not yet recovered. Enter a healing profession, or volunteer your time.

Delight in what remains

Birds sing after a storm; why shouldn't people feel as free to delight in whatever remains to them?

Rose F. Kennedy (1880–1995), mother of John F. Kennedy, 35th president of the United States

Life is full of human tragedies. We lose each other through death or abandonment. Our material possessions are destroyed by storm, or theft, or fire. We lose our jobs and our source of income. Disease strikes and our lives are never the same. Terrorists kill thousands in senseless acts of violence. It's no news that tragedy strikes on a daily basis. But how you respond makes all the difference.

The best response to tragedy is to celebrate what remains, even if it's only the shirt on your back. Survive adversity by delighting in the smallest things – a beautiful vase, a warm meal or the kind words of another human being.

Garden without chemicals

One individual with a digging fork and a small garden can make a difference.

John Harrison, author of *Gardening for the Future of the Earth*

Pesticide use in our homes, in our office buildings and on our food represents a growing health problem. The number of people who have what has come to be called 'chemical sensitivity' or 'environmental illness' is on the rise. If you have a garden, try to handle insect problems in a healthy way, without using chemical pesticides.

Use a saucer of beer to attract and remove slugs. Plant a border of marigolds to repel insects. Or purchase 'beneficial bugs' to remove harmful pests such as aphids, caterpillars, moths or mealy bugs. Do some research on the Web, and in books on organic gardening, for information pertaining to where you live.

Practise exuberance

Exuberance is beauty.
William Blake, poet and painter (1757–1827)

Don't be cool and calculating. Don't withhold your enthusiasm for life.
Instead, be like a baby and absolutely squeal for joy. Dance wildly
around your living room, make a fool of yourself and laugh until the
tears run down your cheeks. Give someone you love a huge bunch of
flowers, and kiss your mother for no reason. Don't stop there – roll
down the car windows and sing your heart out.

   Holding back your exuberance makes you old before your time. It
may even make you sick as well. If you don't express your joy, you may
forget how to be joyful. Express your joy full out at least once a day. Not
only will you feel better, but you'll look better too!

Make your money work socially

Most investors operate on the concept that investing is an act without real world consequences. Nothing could be further from the truth.
Ami L. Domini, author of *Socially Responsible Investing*

If you have savings and investments, make your assets grow while simultaneously helping to create a better world. Integrate your personal values and societal concerns with your investment decisions through socially responsible investing.

Some investment companies offer mutual funds that screen for various business practices or products that you find incompatible with your values. For instance, you can invest in funds that exclude tobacco, or in companies with a clean record on the environment, or in funds that invest in low-income communities. Search the Web for socially responsible investing funds. Most perform as well as, or better than, regular funds.

Listen to emotion

So when you are listening to somebody, completely, attentively, then you are listening not only to the words, but also to the feeling of what is being conveyed, to the whole of it, not part of it.

Jiddu Krishnamurti, philosopher (1895–1986)

To communicate well you need to listen well, and that means paying attention to more than words alone. Notice how the person you're speaking to holds their body. Do you observe any tension? Do they make eye contact in a natural way or are they having difficulty looking at you? What emotion do you sense behind their words? Is it fear, contentment, anger?

Learning to take in the whole of what is being conveyed will help you better understand what someone says, as well as become a more compassionate listener and friend.

Dance

Our ancestors danced till they disappeared in the dance, till they felt the full force of spirit unleashing their souls.

Gabrielle Roth, author of *Sweat Your Prayers*

Dancing is free. Dance under the full moon, dance at dawn, dance at sundown. Dance naked in the privacy of your living room. Put on music and move however you want to move. That's dancing – no need for lessons, to be beautiful or have a great body, be young or talented.

Let your dance be personal and private or, if you want, communal and shared. Your dance can be whatever you want it to be. The main thing is to be sure to bring dance into your life. Dance at least once a week, if not daily. If you're feeling down, or stuck, it's absolutely the best medicine.

Have that difficult conversation

What makes these situations so hard to face? It's our fear of the consequences – whether we raise the issue or try to avoid it.
Douglas Stone, author of *Difficult Conversations*

If you've been putting off a difficult conversation with a partner, another family member or your boss, it's probably hurting you more than the actual conversation ever could. You may need to end a relationship, bring up the past with an abuser, or raise something equally frightening and challenging.

Before you have the conversation, get help from a counsellor, or consult self-help books. You don't have to go in there without support. Let a close friend or therapist know what you are about to do. After the conversation, be sure you have a friend or counsellor to talk to about your experience.

Commit to change

The need for change bulldozed a road down the centre of my mind.
Maya Angelou, poet (b. 1928)

Change of any kind can be exciting or frightening. The fun kind we pursue; the frightening kind we tend to put off.

If you need to quit smoking, lose weight or leave a relationship, let the reality sink in. Let any feelings emerge — fear, anger or whatever else is on your mind. Then mentally close the door of the past behind you. Now you're going to go forward, one step at a time, and change what you have to change. If you have to stop smoking, develop a plan: see your doctor, get a prescription, sign up at a stop-smoking clinic. If you have to end a relationship, get support from a friend or therapist. Once you commit to change, your fear and anger will lessen, and your hope and energy will increase.

Bird-watch

I hope you love birds too. It is economical. It saves going to heaven.
Emily Dickinson, poet (1830–86)

Regardless of where you live, bird-watching is one of the most frugal
and funs things you can ever do.

Buy a bird feeder and hang it near your window. Fill it with birdseed,
pull up a chair and enjoy one of nature's most beautiful displays.

Get a bird book and a notepad. Write down each species you identify.
Over time you'll get better at noticing differences in colour and markings.
If you want to attract a wider variety of birds, find out what kind of
feeder works best for each type of bird. If you want to extend your
relationship with birds, you might want to build a birdhouse and watch
nest-building in your own back yard. Bird-watching can be addictive, so
be careful it doesn't take over your life.

Benefit seven generations

Our past is our present, our present is our future, and our future is seven generations past and present.

Haudenosaunee teaching, quoted in Winona LaDuke's *All Our Relations*

The Haudenosaunee is a Native American tribe, also known as the Six Nations of the Iroquois. 'Seven generations' is the term used to describe the belief that all activities need to take into account the needs and requirements of seven generations into the future. This includes taking care of the members of the tribe, its descendants, and 'Mother Earth' and her ecosystem.

Would you change your day-to-day decisions about how you live, or what you spend, if you considered the effect on seven future generations? What could you do with your life that would benefit at least seven generations to come?

Communicate in person

Electric communication will never be a substitute for the face of someone who with his or her soul encourages another person to be brave and true.

Charles Dickens, novelist (1812–70)

You probably have access to round-the-clock, instantaneous communication by land-phone, mobile phone and email. It's easy to put off visiting someone when you can talk, or email, as often as you like. But it's important to make time to see your friends and family in person. The smiley faces and other codes you may use in email speak volumes as to what is lacking in your 'electric communication'. You miss the nuance in the voice, the twinkle in the eye, the beginnings of a smile, the brush of a hand or a good hug.

Don't rely on email and phones as a substitute for communicating with someone in person. Make time in your life to be with the people you love.

Don't kill your dreams

To kill your dreams because they are irresponsible is to be irresponsible to yourself. Credibility lies with you and God – not with a vote of friends and acquaintances.

Julia Cameron, author of *The Artist's Way*

If you have a dream – to paint, to sing, to write as a career – you may have to contend with disapproval from friends and relatives. They may think you're irresponsible, and your aspirations frivolous. They may insist that only certain lifestyles are acceptable: lawyer, doctor or other professional; those careers that guarantee the most power and status. However, you have the power to decide what's important to you, and what your responsibilities are.

It's important to hold your own and maintain your dreams. Work out a way to make them happen. Use your creativity to find a way to support yourself and practise your art. If you believe in yourself, then others will too.

Recycle

Use it up, wear it out, make it do, or do without.

New England proverb

The case for recycling is strong. It requires a trivial amount of your time. It saves money and reduces pollution. It creates more jobs than land-filling or incineration. It helps save trees. And recycling reduces your need to dump your rubbish in someone else's back yard. Your glass, plastic and paper are put to good use.

Get your kids involved and teach them how to sort recyclables and how to prepare them for pick-up or drop-off. Try to reuse items within your household as much as possible. Recycling is good medicine for the universe, and it makes you feel good that you're helping it to heal.

Sing

Whatever the reason, be it physical, emotional, psychological or spiritual in nature, singing is powerful.

Carolyn Sloan, author of *Finding Your Voice*

Do you sing alone in the car along with your radio? How about in the shower? If you don't sing, what's holding you back? Singing releases tension, cheers you up, lifts your spirits and heals your soul. Singing is powerful. You don't have to have a 'good voice' or even sing in key – just belt out a song whenever you feel like it.

For additional fun, sing with friends. This doesn't need to be an expensive night out at your local karaoke bar. Have a pot-luck dinner and a 'sing-along' at home. You and your friends can have just as much fun there, with good food, a guitar and lots of laughter.

Teach your kids about money

Communicate with children, as they grow, about your values concerning money and how to save it, make it grow, and most importantly how to spend it wisely.

Paul Richard, executive director, Institute of Consumer Financial Education

David Owen, author of *The First National Bank of Dad*, discovered a way to teach his children about money that's not punitive and that rewards responsible spending. He set up a bank for them at home, with unusually high rates of return. In this way they were able to double or triple their allowance. Through this method he also taught them about investments and charitable giving.

Find an innovative way to teach your children the value of saving. Help them have good values when it comes to consumerism and spending. If you need advice, check out books on kids' money and select one that's right for you and your family.

Don't shrink yourself

Your playing small doesn't serve the world. There's nothing enlightened about shrinking so that other people won't feel insecure around you.
Nelson Mandela, former president of South Africa (b. 1918)

Do you have a friend or family member who feels diminished by your intelligence, your creativity or your knowledge? Do you hide your abilities and talents, or stay in the background, in order to prevent a jealous reaction in your friends? Do you have dreams and ideas that you keep to yourself because they may challenge those closest to you?

The price you pay for hiding your talents is steep. You're being dishonest in not being your true self, and you're withholding your gifts from the world. Playing small doesn't serve you, or your friends. Be the best person you can be, for yourself and for the rest of the world.

Chant

Chant is singing our prayers. Chant is vocal meditation. Chant is the breath made audible in tone. Chant is discovering spirit in sound.
Robert Gass, author of *Chanting*

You may be familiar with chanting through Gregorian chant; through Buddhist or Hindu chant; or, if you're into popular music, through contemporary 'Asian fusion'. Chanting is a powerful method for freeing the body and mind, and if you haven't tried it yourself you may want to explore its many benefits.

Listen to CDs of chanting and imitate what you hear. Or visit a Buddhist or Hindu temple and ask to learn. The regular practice of chanting relaxes your muscles, lowers your blood pressure, reduces stress levels, sharpens your mind and supports your overall health and well-being.

Affirm your completeness

Your completeness must be understood by you and experienced in your thoughts as your own personal reality.
Wayne Dyer, author of *There's a Spiritual Solution to Every Problem*

We live in cultures where advertising invades our lives 24/7. The message of most advertising is that you're lacking something, and that the product being advertised will make you whole. It's important to overcome that basic message by meditating on your own completeness.

Find a quiet moment and close your eyes. Affirm that you are not an apprentice human being in need of approval by an outside authority. Affirm that you are not lacking in beauty, health or material possessions. Affirm to yourself that you are complete and whole. Affirm to yourself, and the universe, that you are perfect just as you are.

Work out your disagreements

Got disagreements? Work 'em out ...

Paul Simon (b. 1941), in a song entitled 'Old', from the album *You're the One*

If you have serious disagreements with a friend, family or colleague, and you want to maintain your relationship, find a way to work them out. If you feel stuck, get help from a mediator – a third person whom you both trust. Be willing to understand the other person's concerns and point of view, and share your own, without blaming or putting the other person down. Express your feelings openly and encourage the other person to do so as well. It's easy to express anger, but if you're afraid let the other person know that too.

Living with underlying tension, because of ongoing disagreements, is stressful and complicates your life. To simplify your life, keep your relationships as open and harmonious as possible.

Use cloth nappies

It's the best choice you can make for the health of your baby and the planet.

Janet McConnell, author of 'The Joy of Cloth Diapers', *Mothering Magazine*

Disposable nappies take up a large proportion of our landfill sites. If you have a baby, use plain cloth nappies — for yourself, your baby and the environment. Either make your own or buy them (you'll need about two to four dozen). They aren't that difficult to handle, once you get used to them and develop a routine.

For a number of reasons, cloth nappies are best for you and your baby. They're softer and more comfortable. It's easier for you to tell if your baby needs changing. Babies wearing cloth nappies get potty-trained earlier. And yes, you save a lot of money. If you don't want to use pins, try one of the Velcro covers that are available. If you simply can't handle washing cloth nappies, use a nappy service — you'll still save money.

Value your democracy

I don't know exactly what democracy is. But we need more of it.

Anonymous Chinese student, during protests in Tiananmen Square, Beijing, 1989

Living in a democracy is a gift, but it's also a responsibility. It's important to vote, but there are lots of other ways to participate as a citizen.

Know what's going on at the national and local level. Read, watch and listen to sources of news that you trust. Find alternative news sources at your news-stand or on the Web. Get involved in politics in your city or town. Let your elected officials know how you feel about issues concerning you and your neighbours. Write letters to the editor of your local newspaper on topics you care about. Start a petition to change a situation you don't like. There are so many ways to participate – choose what appeals to you. Don't take your democracy for granted.

Compost

Compost is more than a fertilizer, more than a soil conditioner. It is a symbol of continuing life.
Grace Gershuny, author of *The Rodale Book of Composting*

Composting takes place naturally in every forest, swamp and prairie in the world, as vegetable matter decays and fertilizes the soil. Our modern composting is simply a speeded-up version of a natural process.

If you're a gardener, try recycling your garden and food waste to make your own compost. It's great for the environment as well as your soil, and you'll never have to buy topsoil or fertilizer again. You can buy composters at garden centres or get instructions to build your own. Be willing to learn a little about how composting works, from books or a friendly gardener in your neighbourhood. Experiment with various methods until you find whatever works for you.

Be careful what you swallow

Be careful what you swallow. Chew!
Gwendolyn Brooks, poet (1917–2000)

You have opportunities to hear, watch and read vast amounts of information on a daily basis. But when it comes to information it's important to bite off only what you can chew.

Don't overwhelm yourself with more than you can comprehend. Develop your ability to question what you take in, and to discriminate hype from fact. Critical thinking is essential in our information- and advertising-driven world. When analyzing what you read, hear or see, consider the source and its interests and agendas. Don't accept everything as true just because it's on the evening news. Learn to rely on your own intelligence.

Be adventurous

Adventure is worthwhile in itself.
Amelia Earhart, aviator (1897–1937)

The road to audacity is often the road to excitement and fulfilment. Do you watch adventure movies and read accounts of travel to exotic locations, yet cling to the safety and comfort of your living-room sofa? Open your life to adventure – whether it be travelling to places you've never been to or simplifying your life by dramatically changing the way you live.

Clinging to material possessions and comfort keeps you stuck in a predictable, safe and unexciting life. Be willing to try new things and explore the unknown: in your internal life, in the way you live and in your work. Make your entire life an adventure.

Renew your love

Love doesn't just sit there like a stone; it has to be made, like bread,
remade all the time, made new.
Ursula K. Le Guin, author (b. 1929)

You fall in love, enter a committed relationship and
assume that your love will continue. Unfortunately,
love does not stay frozen in time. Like a rare flower,
love takes daily care and nurture. Today is not the same
as yesterday, nor will it be the same as tomorrow. Because you and
your partner are constantly evolving and changing, you need to recreate
your love on a daily basis.

Express your love often, in small ways and more significant ways,
both verbally and non-verbally. Be willing to give your undivided
attention as an expression of your love. Keep your love life alive and
exciting. Concentrate on the things you love about the other person, not
on their faults. Don't take your spouse or lover for granted.

Share your knowledge

If you have knowledge, let others light their candles in it.
Margaret Fuller, author and transcendentalist (1810–50)

It's said that 'knowledge is power'. Because you live in a competitive world, you may have a tendency to hold on to your knowledge. Giving it away freely may seem foolish, when you could charge for it.

However, this mercenary approach to knowledge makes your heart miserly. Instead, share your knowledge freely – and your business and relationships will improve. By lifting everyone around you, you will benefit by having colleagues who care about you and appreciate your generosity. You will help create a loving work atmosphere in which everyone enjoys the free exchange of knowledge. Instead of competing, you and your colleagues will be able to do your best work together and will improve both your work and your relationships.

Barter, exchange and buy together

When the stranger says: 'What is the meaning of this city?' what will you answer? 'We all dwell together to make money from each other' or 'This is a community'?

T. S. Eliot, poet (1888–1965)

Consider that you and your neighbours probably own household possessions that you might be able to share. Typical items are lawnmowers, garden tools and power saws or drills. Start a tool exchange with a group of your neighbours or friends. If you need to buy an expensive tool, see if others are interested in sharing the expense and owning it communally.

Bartering is also a great way to save money. Have a meeting with a group who are interested in bartering. Let everyone say what they are willing to share and what they would like to receive in return. Some suggestions for barter include hair-cutting skills, massages, sewing and garment repair, gardening, care repair, computer training, word processing and baby-sitting.

Do less of what doesn't matter

I already knew simplicity is about power. Simplicity is the power to do less (of what doesn't matter). Simplicity is the power to do more (of what does matter).

Bill Jensen, author of *The Simplicity Survival Handbook*

Bill Jensen writes about simplicity in the workplace. He suggests working with management to cut down on endless meetings, inter-office email and other day-to-day time-wasters that leave you frustrated and unsatisfied with your work life. He advocates giving workers the information they need to do their jobs, and the authority to adjust that information to take care of their responsibilities.

Get together with your colleagues and see if you can suggest a way to make your work life simpler. Make a plan and present it to the management. Not all managers or business owners will be open to suggestions, but if you present your ideas as a way to improve their business your proposals may get their ear.

Teach

I touch the future. I teach.

Christa McAuliffe, teacher and astronaut (1948–1986)

If you have skills and knowledge, consider sharing them as a professional teacher. If you are a young person, consider a teaching career; if you are middle-aged, tired of what you're doing and feeling unfulfilled, you might also consider a move into teaching – the world needs good teachers who are mature and who have life experience as well as knowledge.

If you teach, you probably won't get wealthy, but your days will be rich with the satisfaction that you are helping young people get a good start in life. Helping children grow and learn means directly working to shape the future. Remember how the teachers in your past influenced you deeply and changed you for ever. Be that person who makes a difference in someone else's life.

Weep with your whole heart

Those who don't know how to weep with their whole heart don't know how to laugh either.

Golda Meir, former prime minister of Israel (1898–1978)

Sometimes you just feel like crying. When that happens, don't hold back. Let your sadness, grief or happiness pour out.

The ability to feel deeply enriches your life, making you more compassionate and loving towards others. Crying relieves pent-up emotion, providing a form of natural release; it even clears your sinuses. If you're a man, it's important to validate your right to cry. If you're a woman, don't accept any criticism that you're being too emotional. Feel free to cry alone or in public, and in front of loved ones. Your tears will help others to be able to express their emotions freely.

Do what you think you can't do

You gain strength, courage and confidence by every experience in which you really stop to look fear in the face. You must do the thing which you think you cannot do.

Eleanor Roosevelt, former First Lady of the United States (1884–1962)

Think of something you would like to do that you feel is beyond you – beyond your skills, your intelligence, your age or your gender. Do you want to climb a mountain, sail a boat or run a marathon? Do you want to write a book, run for political office or give a talk before a large crowd of people?

First, feel the fear. It's okay to be afraid. Then start planning how you might accomplish what you want to do. If it's speaking before a crowd, start by practising in front of a few friends. In taking some small steps, in spite of your fear, you will gain courage and confidence. If you are willing to look fear in the face, you will be able to do much more than you ever imagined.

Study nature

Study nature, love nature, stay close to nature. It will never fail you.
Frank Lloyd Wright (1869–1959)

It's great to be in nature, to enjoy a walk on a sunny day or to go camping for a weekend with friends or family. What makes it even more delightful is knowing about your surroundings.

Try to educate yourself about your environment. Know the trees that grow in your area and how to identify them by their bark and leaves. Know the birds by their feathers and song, and the animals by their fur and habits. Know the flowers by their colour, shape and perfume. Know which plants are poisonous and which are beneficial.

By understanding nature, and taking the time to learn about her endless variety, you'll feel closer to the earth and comforted by the beauty of all life.

Make the most of your life

Life is what we make it, always has been, always will be.
Grandma Moses, primitive artist (1860–1961)

It's easy to slide through your days, then weeks, then months, then years, without making the most of the time you have. Life is not something that happens to you – rather, it is something you create on a moment-by-moment basis. With all the stresses of modern life, it's easy to forget that you are in control of what you do.

Take a moment and close your eyes. Ask yourself if you have lived your life as fully as you would have liked. If the answer is no, ask yourself what you could have done differently. Meditate on the fact that you are in control of what you choose to do *now*. No matter what your age, it's not too late. Starting from this moment, decide to make the most of the rest of your life.

Don't wait for leaders

Do not wait for leaders; do it alone, person to person.
Mother Teresa, Catholic nun (1910–97)

If you have a problem in your community that needs addressing, it's natural to look to your elected officials to take care of the matter. But the wheels of local government can move very slowly.

Try getting together with some friends who have the same concerns and brainstorming how you might address the problem. If you have homeless people on the street, and your city council is not doing enough to take care of them, start a homeless shelter in a local church that is willing to donate space. If local teenagers are getting into trouble because they don't have enough to do, start an after-school programme run by volunteers.

Shed care and worry

By being content with little and not giving a rap for what the neighbours think, one can attain a very large measure of freedom, shedding care and worry in a trice.

John Blofeld, author of *Bodhisattva of Compassion*

The material and financial aspects of your life can generate a lot of worry and stress. Working very hard to make the money to buy possessions, shopping for possessions and then managing them takes a huge toll on your energy. If you can take the radical step of being satisfied with very little money or possessions, a huge part of your worries will dissipate.

Because material possessions are an indication of success, you will have to come to terms with how you define success in your life. You will also need to disregard what others think of your decision. But you may have discovered the secret of a worry-free life and, if you can maintain your focus on how carefree you feel, what others think won't bother you at all.

Live green

It's really very simple and requires no expert knowledge or complex skills. Here's the answer. Consume less. Share more. Enjoy life.
Penny Kemp and Derek Wall, authors of *A Green Manifesto for the 1990s*

The Green movement is a catch-all phrase that encompasses Green parties around the world, the ecology movement, the conservation movement, the environmental movement and the peace movement. If you want to live green, you can find kindred spirits in any of these groups or just experiment with living a simpler life.

To do this, cut down on your consumption; be more society- and community-oriented; and by all means enjoy living on a day-to-day basis. If you are living green, you are choosing to live in harmony with nature and the planet as much as possible. Be kind to yourself – it's a work in progress.

Love all

Love every leaf, every ray of light.
Love the animals, love the plants, love each separate thing.
Loving all, you will perceive the mystery of God in all.
Fyodor Dostoevsky, novelist (1821–81)

Dostoevsky had it right: love cures all. When you are self-absorbed in your own thoughts, spending time pondering your problems or speculating on what's going to happen in the future, it's easy to forget about 'the mystery of God'.

The next time you are struggling with your emotions or trying to solve issues in your life, take a few minutes and focus intently on what's around you at that particular moment. Consciously generate a sense of love for whomever or whatever it is. See if this doesn't soften your heart, ease your worries and lift your mind beyond your everyday concerns, and towards something bigger than yourself. Let yourself merge with this larger sense of God, however you think of him or her.

Dematerialize Christmas

Christmas is a school for consumerism – in it we learn to equate delight with materialism. We celebrate the birth of One who told us to give everything to the poor by giving each other motorized tie racks.
Bill McKibben, in *Christianity Today*, December 1996

Christmas celebrates the birth of Christ. How easy it is to forget the reason why we have the holiday in the first place. So much frenzy takes place around gift-buying that Christ gets lost to Christmas.

If you celebrate Christmas – whether or not you're Christian – take some time to recall the life of the historical Christ and to remind yourself of what He stood for and taught. He certainly taught that we should share our wealth with those less fortunate. Try to make your celebration of His birthday more spiritual than material, by doing something for the homeless in your city or spending the afternoon in a soup kitchen serving food to those in need.

Don't confuse symbols and things

Any so-called material thing that you want is merely a symbol: you want it not for itself, but because it will content your spirit for the moment.
Mark Twain, author (1835–1910)

The next time you are buying a higher-priced item, like a car, ask yourself what this purchase means to you. A car may mean a lot more to you than mere transportation: you might think of it as a symbol of your sexuality, your age or your status in life (whether you have that status or not).

If you want to have a better sex life, feel younger or feel pleased with your position in life, don't turn to possessions to supply what can only be obtained by other means. Learn how to be a better lover by loving; revamp your attitude towards life, if you want to feel younger; and examine what really matters to you, if you want to feel pleased with your status.

Don't be hip

We bustle around trying to create the impression that we are hip, imperturbable, omniscient, in perfect control, when in fact we are awkward and scared and bewildered.

Martha Beck, author of *Expecting Adam*

When you're lured into being like the cool, controlled, perfect people you see in advertisements, it's easy to forget that what you're imitating is just an illusion.

It takes a lot of energy to be hip and cool. You have to wear the right clothes, look good, appear bored, and be in complete control of your situation – and, by all means, not express any emotion that might make you seem vulnerable.

If you have been tempted to be hip or cool, ask yourself if the energy and stress are worth it. Relax. Express your emotions freely and honestly. Give up being hip, and embrace being human.

Have a family dinner

The family is one of nature's masterpieces.

George Santayana, philosopher, poet and humanist (1863–1952)

The dinner table used to be where the family gathered for the evening meal. After the dishes were cleared, it became the place to do homework. Later in the evening it might hold a sewing project, or the monthly bills. With our overly busy lives, the dinner table is now a dumping place for unopened mail and stray items. With everyone's conflicting schedule, it's often impossible to gather everyone for a family dinner. Takeout meals are eaten on the run, or frozen dinners are wolfed down in front of the TV.

Clear off the table and insist on a family dinner where everyone contributes. Talk about the need for family time and commit to having a home-made meal together at least once a week. Use the time to talk about what's going on in your lives.

Live independently

There is no dignity quite so impressive, and no independence quite so important, as living within your means.

Calvin Coolidge, 30th president of the United States (1872–1933)

Living with debt takes its toll – physically, emotionally and spiritually. You are in financial and psychological bondage to others, whether it's a bank, a credit-card company or another individual. Even if you're one of the rare people who don't use credit cards, you still may be using borrowed money in the form of a car payment or a mortgage.

If so, make sure you're not 'mortgage poor', or over-extended with your car payment. If you are, downsize your home and drive a less expensive car. If you have credit-card debt, stop using your cards. Pay off the balance, and buy everything else on a cash basis. Put off making purchases until you can afford them. You may cringe at the idea of having less or going without, when credit is so easy to obtain, but consider how wonderful it would feel to be living independently, free and clear of debt.

Don't seek revenge

An eye for an eye only leads to more blindness.

Margaret Atwood, novelist (b. 1939)

When you feel wounded by someone, it's easy to want to lash out and hurt them in return. You may control yourself in the moment, but later, when alone, you may begin to plot your revenge. If you felt humiliated at the time, you may plan to humiliate the other person in the same way. You might imagine that doing this will not only relieve your pain, but will also make you feel triumphant. However, the truth is that you'll gain nothing, you won't feel any better and you'll only contribute to more anger and hatred in the world.

Don't seek revenge. There are many ways to deal with your pain other than by inflicting it on others.

Stop hurrying

Never be in a hurry; do everything quietly and in a calm spirit. Do not lose your inner peace for anything whatsoever, even if your whole world seems upset.

St Frances de Sales, Catholic saint (1567–1622)

Do you rush to get places? Do you hate having to wait? Hurrying can make you feel important and part of the excitement of life. But these are false feelings. Hurrying doesn't result in better productivity or help you make a positive contribution. Instead, it makes you inefficient, irritable, prone to mistakes, exhausted and self-centred. You also double your odds of getting high blood pressure, a stroke or a heart attack.

Decide to stay focused in the moment, and work on one project at a time. Regardless of what the rest of the world is doing, work and live at a pace that keeps you centred and whole.

Live in a smaller space

More rooms, bigger space and vaulted ceilings do not necessarily give us what we need in a home.

Sarah Susanka, author of *The Not So Big House*

Take a tour of your house or apartment and determine how much you use each room. Do you rarely use the dining room, and prefer to eat in the kitchen? If you have a family room, does your living room stay unused except for holidays or special occasions? Do you have an extra bedroom filled with boxes of stuff you haven't looked at in years?

Catalogue the furniture or storage housed in your unused rooms. To save money and simplify your life, move to a smaller house or apartment. Sell or give away furniture and other items that you don't use on a regular basis. Then make your living space warm and functional.

Realize that your soul doesn't need money

Money is not required to buy one necessity of the soul.
Henry David Thoreau, essayist, poet and naturalist (1817–62)

Your soul needs love, understanding, a spiritual life, compassion for yourself and others, inspiration and meaning. Get a notebook and write about your soul – what it is and how it is expressed in your life.

If you never think of your soul, then write about that and why you don't consider it. Then close your eyes and ask your soul what it needs. Write down whatever your soul answers. See if anything on your list requires money. Use this exercise to shift your focus from money and material possessions to the care of your soul.

Calculate your ecological footprint

There is convincing evidence that above a certain threshold, further consumption adds little to reported quality of life. For example, the percentage of Americans calling themselves 'happy' peaked in 1957 – even though consumption has more than doubled in the meantime.

Nicky Chambers, author of *Sharing Nature's Interest*

Enter 'ecological footprint' in a search engine on the Web and you will get a choice of sites where you can take your own ecological footprint test. The test is an accounting tool that measures your consumption against the Earth's capacity to provide for you. You will learn how big your own ecological footprint is in relation to that of others in the world. This will give you an idea of where to start reducing your impact on the Earth and living a more environmentally friendly life.

Live a good life

There is no shortage of good days. It is good lives that are hard to come by.

Annie Dillard, writer (b. 1945)

What is a good life? Spend some time thinking about exactly what this concept means to you. One ingredient of a good life might be pleasure; another ingredient might be bringing joy to other people. You might consider that having a purpose and achieving your goals is essential. Or you might feel that a good life is one in which you are a loving person, and are loved in return.

Try to imagine what would have to happen for you to feel that you were living a good life. Then live your days to achieve that ideal.

Pay attention to the moon

Right down to the level of individual cells, the lunar wind is blowing and bringing all living creatures into vibrant motion.

Johanna Paungger, author of *Moon Time*

When the moon is new (or dark), set your intention for something you would like to manifest – perhaps healing for yourself or someone else, or a new relationship. As the waxing crescent appears in the night sky, see this as the first sign of the manifestation of your intent.

When the moon reaches its fullness, meditate on what it is that you desire and look for signs and visions of your way into the future. Let your intention flow out into the universe. As the moon wanes, visualize your intention coming to fruition for the benefit of yourself and everyone else.

Take your power

Power can be taken, but not given. The process of the taking is empowerment in itself.

Gloria Steinem, journalist and feminist (b. 1934)

'Taking your power' is not about having power over others. It is about setting boundaries and acting on behalf of your own needs, in a way that does not cause harm to others.

Think about your friends, your family, your boss or your teachers. Are you taking your power in these relationships in a positive way? Are you stating your needs and opinions clearly, without apology? Are you ensuring that any compromises you make are in line with your values? In order to take your power, you have to be clear about what you feel and think of the people and situations that affect your life. Spend some time clarifying your thoughts and feelings on a daily basis.

Speak your mind

Stand before the people you fear and speak your mind – even if your voice shakes.

Maggie Kuhn, activist for older Americans (1905–95)

Things may happen that you disagree with, but you may be too frightened to speak up. If your boss makes a racist remark at work, or a friend tells a sexist joke, or you're at a meeting and you want to articulate your views, you may find yourself bursting to express yourself, but too afraid to say anything. However, by not speaking up you cause yourself tremendous harm, and the world loses your contribution.

Even though it may be difficult, speak with a shaking voice if you have to. You will gain the courage over time always to speak your mind – and your heart.

Keep a schedule

A schedule defends from chaos and whim. It is a net for catching days. It is a scaffolding on which a worker can stand and labour with both hands at sections of time.
Annie Dillard, writer (b. 1945)

If you have a job, you follow your employer's schedule for at least eight hours of your day. But your other 16 unplanned hours may be disorganized. If you are freelance, or if you are a stay-at-home mother, you may balk at the idea of having a schedule because it sounds unnecessary and overly regimented. But keeping to a schedule will keep you focused on your life goals, and will make much easier daily decisions about what to do when.

   If you don't have a good schedule, experiment with creating one that meets your unique needs. Keep adjusting it if it isn't working quite right.

Don't wait to improve the world

How wonderful it is that nobody need wait a single moment before starting to improve the world.

Anne Frank, holocaust victim (1929–45)

Anne Frank's words are especially moving to us because of her tremendous courage in the face of horrific circumstances. How much easier for us it would be to take her advice.

Every morning think about what you can do to improve the world in the next 24 hours. If you go for a walk in the park, consider picking up and disposing of any rubbish you may find along the way. Remember to smile and be kind to shop assistants and anyone else whom you may encounter. If you find yourself feeling angry with someone, don't lash out. Try to be compassionate and recognize that they are struggling with life just as you are. In small ways you have the opportunity to improve the world in every single moment.

Be willing to compromise

Lasting change is a series of compromises. And compromise is all right, as long your values don't change.

Jane Goodall, primatologist (b. 1934)

You're probably familiar with people who insist on doing things their way. You may even be one of those people. You know it's important to compromise, but how do you compromise without harming yourself?

The answer is by knowing your boundaries and trying to accommodate the other person's needs as best you can. If your partner wants to eat Italian and you are on a low-carb diet, pick a different restaurant that you may not like as much, but which offers pasta as well as other choices. Be willing to work to make the situation the best for everyone involved.

Give up people-pleasing

*The truth is that 'people pleasing' is a sweet-sounding name for what,
to many people, actually is a serious psychological problem.*
Harriet B. Braiker, author of *The Disease to Please*

Do you say 'yes' when you really want to say 'no?' Do you have an
overwhelming need for the approval of others? If so, you're probably
hiding under your 'niceness'. You have the mistaken notion that if you
always think of others first you'll be protected from rejection or abuse.

By not learning how to handle difficult emotions, and by being
attached to seeing yourself as a people-pleaser, you leave yourself open
to manipulation. You may also be so externally focused that you lose
track of your real thoughts and feelings. If you are a people-pleaser, get
help to recover. Learn to balance your own needs with those of others.

Learn to exhale

Through the years I have found it wonderful to acquire, but it is also
wonderful to divest. It's rather like exhaling.
Helen Hayes, actress (1900–93)

You could be 'turning blue' holding on to things that have outlived their
usefulness. By not exhaling, or divesting, you're causing stagnant energy
to accumulate in your home, and in your life.

If you show less attachment to your possessions, you'll be able both
to acquire and divest easily. You'll have the sense of freedom that comes
from being able to let go. You won't feel burdened and oppressed by
accumulated possessions that you're not using. Look round your house
for unused items and practise 'exhaling' once a month.

Write your own epitaph

If you wish to live, you must first attend your own funeral.
Katherine Mansfield, author (1888–1923)

What would you want written on your tombstone? What would you want said at your funeral? These may sound like morbid questions, but your answers will give you guidance for living the rest of your life. For it is only by accepting the reality of your death that you can really feel alive in the present.

Take an afternoon and contemplate your answers. Would you want people to say that you lived a good life; that you were generous; a good partner or parent; a loving friend, sister or brother? What special quality would you want people to mention? Begin now to create a life that you and others can celebrate.

Create the intention for happiness

But does not happiness come from the soul within?
Honoré de Balzac, novelist (1799–1850)

The single most important ingredient in achieving happiness is having the *intention* to be happy. However, creating that intention may cause some resistance. Are you used to struggling or suffering? Is that a part of your identity? If so, then putting this on the table is a good thing. It's time to acknowledge this and let it go.

Sit down and write a list of 30 activities that make you feel happy. Intend to be happy today by doing one of those activities. For example, if smelling flowers fills you with joy, bring some happiness into your life by visiting a botanical garden or buying yourself a bouquet.

Set priorities

The important thing is to be sure you're connected with your inner compass ...

Roger A. Merrill, author of *Life Matters*

It's not unusual to have two sets of priorities. We have wishing priorities and actual priorities. For example, you may sincerely wish to put your health and family first, but continue to eat badly and overwork. Or you may want to get out of debt, but continue to use your credit card.

Write down what you wish your priorities to be – those activities and qualities that you want to take precedence over others. Then write down a brief recap of what you did during the last week. How well are you adhering to your priorities? Asses how you spend your time. If your priorities and your reality are not congruent, start making small changes week by week. Keep track of your progress in a journal.

Shoot for the moon

Shoot for the moon. Even if you miss, you'll land among the stars.
Les Brown, musician (1912–2001)

If you have something you dream of doing, don't do it half-heartedly. As Les Brown says, 'Shoot for the moon!' If you want to go back to college, don't settle for a few courses — get that degree! If you want to live in the country, don't just rent a cottage at weekends. Start looking for land and take the plunge.

Don't sell yourself short. On a regular basis write down your dreams, no matter how outlandish or unattainable they may sound. Don't hold back. Then pick the dream that most excites you — no matter how seemingly impossible. Write down what it would take to achieve it. Start by taking one small step, then another.

Charge less and provide great service

There are two kinds of companies, those that work to try to charge more and those that work to charge less. We will be the second.
Jeff Bezos, founder and CEO of Amazon.com (b. 1964)

If you are in business for yourself, take advice from the wildly successful founder of Amazon.com and make customer service, and low prices, the two cornerstones of your company.

If you have greed as your motivation, you'll spread bad energy out into the world. Instead, try to imagine your company as one you would like to patronize. Be someone your customers can trust. When you set prices, think of their bank account as well as your own. Over time your goodwill and excellent service will come back to you in the form of a steady income and repeat customers. And you'll be happier and more fulfilled in your work.

Never go to bed angry

Never go to bed mad. Stay up and fight.
Phyllis Diller, comedian (b. 1917)

Great comedians get us to laugh at ourselves while they deliver a little wisdom on the side. You get the joke, but something stays in your mind. In this case, you're reminded that anger is not something to hold on to and let fester over several days. It's not good to turn a cold back to your bed partner, or to punish him or her with your angry silence for days or weeks. Better to have the courage to 'stay up and fight'. Of course, Phyllis Diller is joking and doesn't mean you actually need to fight.

Instead, work it out with your partner – communicate your anger in the most positive way you can, and keep the connection open between you. If you can't resolve your differences before bed, kiss and make an appointment to continue tomorrow.

Don't drown in technology

Technology is so much fun, but we can drown in our technology.
Daniel J. Boorstin, historian (b. 1914)

The latest gadgets are fun to use and explore, but it's important to keep your distance from them as well. The constant hum of electronic devices – televisions, DVDs, VCRs, computers, hand-held planners, mobile phones, fax machines, stereos, boom boxes and home appliances – will drown out the sounds of the birds chirping in the morning, the wind blowing through the trees or a pencil drawing on rough paper.

Technology is mesmerizing and addictive, but be sure to plan days away from its electromagnetic fields. Go out into nature and leave your mobile phone behind. Or just turn everything off and enjoy the peace and quiet.

Lower your caffeine intake

Widespread caffeine use explains a lot about the twentieth century.
Greg Egan, science-fiction writer (b. 1961)

Our pace of life is so demanding that caffeine has become our fuel for the 21st century.

Caffeine – in the form of coffee, tea, chocolate, over-the-counter drugs and soft drinks – is a nice stimulant in very small doses (perhaps the equivalent of one cup of coffee a day). The problem comes from taking in large amounts of caffeine throughout the day, to the point where you may become addicted. If you stop, you may even get withdrawal headaches.

Caffeine can affect your hormone balance and your sleep patterns, and increases your risk of certain health disorders such as osteoporosis, ulcers, PMT, hypertension and heartburn. Try to cut down on your daily intake, or cut caffeine out completely. Explore healthy ways to energize yourself, including exercise, hydration using non-caffeinated beverages, and taking vitamins and herbal supplements.

Relate to what's happening now

As we practise, what grows in our life is this: first, our realization that there is nothing but being in relationship to whatever is happening in each moment; and second, our growing commitment to this relationship.
Charlotte Joko Beck, author of *Everyday Zen*

We are a restless lot. We're always searching for something outside ourselves, and for something to happen in the future. But what we're looking for may be right in front of us — in this very moment.

Notice what's going on right now. Where are you sitting reading this book? Are others present? How do you feel emotionally, and physically? Are you reading, but thinking of many other things at the same time? Take a moment to feel in relationship to the people around you, the furniture you are sitting on, the room you find yourself in, the trees outside, the birds chirping, the sun or the rain, the moon and the stars. Be engaged with, and in relationship to, what's happening right now.

Cultivate your artistic life

Creativity can be described as letting go of certainties.
Helen Keller, deaf-and-blind writer (1880–1968)

There's an old American saying, 'The only things certain in life are death and taxes.' This is probably true. So attempting to create other certainties is a futile undertaking.

If you want to be creative, at some point you'll have to make a leap into the void. You make that leap without any promise of success, or even that there's going to be anything out there for you. The important thing is to not to hang on to the illusion that life will deliver certainty. That will only hold you back. If you want to write a book, face that blank page and write your first sentence. If you want to compete in a marathon, sign up. Will you get published? Maybe; maybe not. Will you win the marathon, or even finish? Hard to say. Will you have an interesting life if you let go of certainty? You can be certain of that!

Don't be ashamed of your mistakes

Sometimes when you innovate, you make mistakes. It is best to admit them quickly, and get on with improving your other innovations.
Steve Jobs, founder and CEO of Apple Computer, Inc. (b. 1955)

If you want to try new things, you're going to make mistakes. If you want to simplify your life, you might make the mistake of downsizing so much that you're unhappy with the result. If you want to have a more spiritual life, you may find yourself in a new community that turns out to be wrong for you.

If you've made a mistake, admit it, learn from it and let it go. It will give you a tremendous amount of information: about your motivation, your strengths and your weaknesses. Mistakes are goldmines, if you're willing to face them head on. Don't let them keep you from pursuing your dreams.

Focus on your mind

Beauty isn't worth thinking about; what's important is your mind. You don't want a fifty-dollar haircut on a fifty-cent head.
Garrison Keillor, writer and radio celebrity (b. 1942)

Beauty is fleeting, and style changes constantly. Don't let beauty and fashion pull you away from your most important tasks in life – to develop your mental intelligence, your emotional intelligence and your spiritual life.

Your mind shapes your reality. How you think creates your life. Take time to read and learn whatever helps make you a better person. Examine the patterns of your thinking. If you see anything negative and harmful, work to create a more positive mind. You'll have a happier and more positive life as a result.

Have biscuits, milk and a nap

Think what a better world it would be if we all, the whole world, had cookies and milk about three o'clock every afternoon and then lay down on our blankets for a nap.

Barbara Jordan, US senator (1936–96)

At first sight, Barbara Jordan's statement seems ludicrous. But, for a moment, imagine how your life would be if you stopped at three o'clock every day, had your milk and biscuits, and took a nap. If you let the idea sink in as an option for an adult, it could change your life.

In centuries past, our ancestors slept more, took their siestas at noon and had their tea at four. Some cultures still take siestas. Why not shut your office door at three, have a snack and stretch out for a little nap? If you can't quite work that out, then approximate. Bring a little sanity and self-nurturing into your day.

Create positive habits

As a twig is bent, the tree inclines.
Virgil, poet (70–19 BCE)

We're all creatures of habit. We wear grooves in our mind from habitual ways of thinking. We wear out our carpet where we walk on it every day. We like our coffee in the morning, and our eggs just so. Our habits get us through the day. But some of our habits are not so beneficial.

Take a moment and think about your habitual negative patterns. Do you have a habit of being jealous if a friend has good fortune? Do you respond with anger when you are afraid? Do you smoke too much?

Our habits bend us in certain directions, and our life then takes on that pattern. Take a look at how your habits are directing your life. If some of them aren't serving you well, work to carve new grooves in positive directions.

Redefine failure

I have not failed. I've just found 10,000 ways that won't work.
Thomas Edison, inventor (1847–1931)

Failure is such a heavy, loaded word. Try redefining the word 'failure' to remove the shame that is so often attached to its meaning. Instead, define failures as ideas or projects that just didn't work out.

If your business venture fails, or you don't make the cut for the team, or you don't pass an exam, you may be disappointed, but these events are not pronouncements on your worth as a human being. If you've experienced a failure, use it as a source of information about how you might improve in the future. Identify errors in thinking, faulty decision-making, or other problems or issues that led to your lack of success. Use your insights to strengthen your future efforts.

Give gifts of service

You give but little when you give of your possessions. It is when you give of yourself that you truly give.
Kahlil Gibran, poet and philosopher (1883–1931)

Birthdays, holidays, weddings – these events usually require you to buy a gift, and it's no surprise that gift-buying takes a large bite out of your budget. A fundamental question to ask is, 'Do I really need to give, and get, more things?'

As an alternative, consider giving gifts of service. Offer to baby-sit, weed the garden or pet-sit while friends are on holiday. Arrange a special outing for the kids. Try hair-cutting, cooking, painting a room or giving a massage. Have your close friends and family members bring a dish to share for supper and discuss feelings about gift-giving. Suggest that, as a group, you try exchanging gifts of service for the coming year.

Purify your mind

Consecrate yourselves to the purification of your minds. Be vigilant, be persevering, be attentive, be thoughtful for your own salvation.

from the *Mahaparinibbana Sutra*, a Buddhist teaching

Buddhists regularly purify their negative actions. No matter what your religion, purification is a wonderful healing and rejuvenating practice.

At the end of your day think about what went well. Spend a moment noting your positive accomplishments. Then take time to review what did not go well. Were you dishonest in a business dealing? Did you speed on the way to work and almost cause an accident? Now take a moment and purify your negative actions. Visualize white light streaming down from above and filling your body, removing all negativity. If you believe in God or a higher power, see the light emanating from them to you. Resolve to avoid negative actions tomorrow.

Be a good leader

You cannot be a good leader unless you find a way of developing and generating courage in yourself, and then 'en-couraging' others.
Robert E. Straub II, author of *The Heart of Leadership*

One of the core values of the simplicity movement is involvement in community. If you've assumed a leadership position in your community – at work, in your social group, in your church or in your local government – how would you rate yourself as a leader? What values do you bring to your role, and what responsibilities do you feel you have?

Leaders have power, but they also have the opportunity to raise everyone around them and to help nurture everyone in their care. How can you do this in your position as leader? Write down ten ways in which you can become a more courageous, compassionate, nurturing and effective leader.

Go beyond intellectual ideals

There are many wonderful concepts and ideals, but if they don't become
who we are, they can become the most fiendish burdens.
Charlotte Joko Beck, **author of** *Nothing Special, Living Zen*

In reading this book, don't beat yourself up with the ideals and concepts
expressed here. They're here to inspire you – and nothing more. If you
pick them up and carry them around in your mind without making them
a part of your life, you'll feel intensely oppressed by their presence and
weighed down by their seeming demands for self-improvement.

When reading these entries, make note of the suggestions and ideas
you want to try, then let the other ones go. Work to integrate the ideas
that appeal into your life, and do that in a way that is uniquely yours.
Intellectual understanding is great, but don't let it burden you. Instead,
rely on your own experience.

Learn from Native Americans

The Navajo universe is alive. It is permeated by subtle life and mind power and operates according to a rhythm and order that culminates in the ideal conditions of Beauty,

Peter Gold, author of *Navajo & Tibetan Sacred Wisdom*

The Navajo, a Native American tribe, honours the land and the four directions. The east is the direction of the dawn and is the thinking direction. When you arise, face east and think before you do anything. When the sun comes up, face the south – the planning direction – and plan what you are going to do today. Do your living facing the west, where you act out your plans and thoughts of the east and south. In the evening, face north and evaluate the outcome of what started in the east. Here you determine to change things for the better, and decide if you're on the right path.

Make your life rich

Develop interest in life as you see it; in people, things, literature, music –
the world is so rich, simply throbbing with rich treasures, beautiful souls
and interesting people.
Henry Miller, author (1891–1980)

As you create a simpler life, you'll begin to realize that you can have an
intensely interesting and amazingly rich life without any money.

The key is to wake up to the beauty and treasures all around you.
For starters, focus on the staggering beauty of the human face: young,
old, black, white, red, yellow, male, female. Simply walk down a busy
street and, without judgement, notice the endless variety and beauty of
the faces passing by. Imagine what their lives are like, and have
compassion for their struggles. And become more interested in your
friends, and get to know them more intimately. Before you get out of
bed, listen intently to the sounds at dawn. Or read a great classic novel.

See by drawing

I never saw an ugly thing in my life: for let the form of an object be what it may – light, shade and perspective will always make it beautiful.
John Constable, landscape painter (1776–1837)

Even if you don't know how to draw, or find yourself intimidated by the very idea, give it a try. No one but you has to see your drawing.

Learn to appreciate the beauty of forms by drawing them without looking at your paper. Pick an object that appeals to you and examine it intently. Then pick up your pen or pencil and begin to draw with your eyes. In other words, don't look down at your pencil and paper – just let your eyes trace the form, and let your hand and pen move accordingly. In this way you'll learn to really look at the world around you. You'll begin to appreciate the infinite variety of shapes and forms that the universe provides to delight your eye and soul. Over time you'll even learn to draw.

Join the human race

The universe is my country and the human race is my tribe.
Kahlil Gibran, poet and philosopher (1883–1931)

It's easy to have an 'us against them' mentality when you live in such a competitive world as ours. You may feel good belonging to an exclusive club. You may find yourself saying things like 'my nation', 'my team', 'my faith' or even 'my race'.

Such divisions are not healthy, for you or the rest of the world. Better to think of yourself as a citizen of the planet. Concern yourself with the health and well-being of everyone in the human race, and the environment in which we all dwell. Meditate on extending kindness to the whole human race.

Be grounded in your spiritual path

We can be lost in cosmic bliss, but still know our zip code.
Ram Dass, author and spiritual teacher (b. 1931)

If you are lucky enough to have gained spiritual insight, in a workshop or retreat, or as a result of hard work over time, you may become disheartened or disillusioned when it doesn't last.

But you can help yourself by understanding that spiritual development is a very long process, and spiritual openings are often followed by the release of old pain, unexpressed anger or grief. Over time you'll understand that spiritual development is a process and a journey, rather than a destination. Be kind to yourself and don't lose heart. Be sure to talk to others on your path about your process. They will appreciate your honesty and candour, and you'll learn that you're not unique in having difficulties.

Learn to sit

It is not so easy to go and sit, and even after you arrive at the zendo and begin sitting, you have to encourage yourself to sit well.
Shunryu Suzuki, Zen Buddhist teacher (1905–71)

Sitting meditation is one of the oldest forms of meditation – and one that the Buddha taught 2,500 years ago. He taught his followers to sit quietly so that they could calm their bodies and minds.

Buddhist meditation is a wonderful practice, regardless of your religion. But before you learn to meditate it's good just to practise sitting quietly. If your days are hectic and full of activity, or you're suffering from stress-related symptoms such as headaches, excessive anger or addictions to stimulants or sedatives, begin to heal by sitting quietly for a short period every morning and evening. If this is helpful to you, pursue formal training in meditation.

Let go of perfectionism

Nearly everyone is afflicted by perfectionism to some degree, and it is easy to see it in others. The challenge is to learn to see it in ourselves.
Cynthia Curnan, author of *The Care and Feeding of Perfectionists*

Perfectionism is a painful habit that's easy to see in others, but hard to identify in yourself. You may celebrate your perfectionism because you think you're devoted to excellence, or just have higher standards than others. Or you may be an unconscious perfectionist as a way to ward off judgement or criticism.

If you admit your perfectionism, you may also find that you have a problem with self-acceptance. You may have difficulty regarding yourself with love and compassion. You may measure your self-worth by what you do, rather than by your qualities. To overcome perfectionism, develop kindness towards yourself and others.

Don't put off starting

The greatest amount of wasted time is the time not getting started.
Dawson Trotman, Evangelical minister (1906–56)

If you want to simplify your life, you need to guard your energy and your time. If you postpone starting the projects you're committed to, you'll complicate your life and drain your energy.

Putting off beginning a project – be it filling out application forms, doing your taxes or simply washing the dishes – takes more of your energy than it saves. While you're diligently avoiding whatever it is that you should be doing, your energy is bound up and not fully available to you. Try to keep your energy clear and free-flowing by starting projects on time.

Learn to knit

Knitting takes unease and supports it with shawls, the way the performers at a big top support a trapeze artist with a net.
Deborah Bergman, author of *The Knitting Goddess*

If you want to simplify, you'll want to slow down. Knitting is a great way to slow down and find balance in a high-tech, fast-paced world. Its benefits are almost too numerous to mention.

Knitting is calming and will relieve your stress. You'll create sweaters for yourself and your family at a fraction of the cost of buying them. You'll enjoy the sensuous pleasure of working with beautiful yarn colours and textures. You'll have a sense of accomplishment when you complete a project. And you can take your knitting with you wherever you go.

Make things last

Most things do not wear out; rather, they are destroyed wilfully so a newer model may be purchased.

Edward H. Romney, author of *Living Well on Practically Nothing*

We live in a throwaway culture. If you're interested in a simpler life, consider repairing your possessions rather than replacing them, or maintaining them so that they last longer.

If your shoes are wearing out, get them resoled. If you have an older car, it may still be cheaper to repair it than take on expensive car payments. If your clothes rip, have them mended or sew them yourself. If you're good with your hands, check out repair manuals from the library and fix your own appliances, furniture and clothes.

Practise mindful speech

Not speaking helps us notice the gift of words.
Gregg Krech, author of *Naikan*

The Buddha recommended that we be mindful of our speech. To do so, try cutting down on jargon and developing a more expressive and precise vocabulary. Instead of chattering, speak when you have something useful to say. Try not to gossip or speak negatively about anyone. Don't stretch the truth to impress or gain advantage. Speak positively and constructively. Have the courage to speak out in situations of injustice. Wait to express your opinion until you have thoroughly considered the subject under discussion.

Practising mindful speech will help you be more useful to others, and feel more balanced and centred in your own life.

Take a yoga class

The postures and breath work that you do in a typical yoga class will change your life.

Katrina Kenison, author of *Meditations from the Mat*

Creating a simpler and more spiritual life will help you slow down, reconnect with your body and improve your health and well-being. Yoga is a wonderful practice for accomplishing all of the above.

There are many ways to find yoga classes and instruction. Try your phone book for listings of yoga studios and schools. For less expensive classes, try your local college, church or neighbourhood school. If you really want to save money, check the TV listings for yoga programmes and follow the actions as you watch. Or find a book at your local library and try teaching yourself. You may want to purchase some inexpensive props, such as blocks, mats, belts and blankets.

Finish what you've started

Nothing is so fatiguing as the eternal hanging on of an uncompleted task.
William James, psychologist (1842–1910)

Having uncompleted tasks hanging over your head can be excruciatingly painful – often more painful than just finishing them. But if your habit is to procrastinate you may not understand this simple truth.

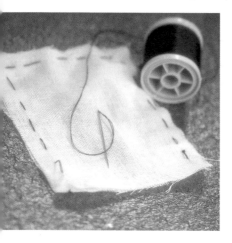

If you have any uncompleted tasks (perhaps a room that's half-painted, an overdue paper for a class, or a sweater you started knitting a year ago), write them down. Then note how having these unfinished tasks makes you feel. You may discover that they cause feelings of guilt, undermine your self-esteem and leave you feeling in bondage to the past. Next, take one unfinished task and complete it. Write down how finishing the task makes you feel. You may find yourself experiencing a sense of freedom, accomplishment and increased energy. Don't let your unfinished tasks drag you down.

Give and get a massage

Massage is an ancient healing art with enormous benefits for all the systems of the body.

Denise Brown, author of *Teach Yourself Massage*

It can feel wonderful to get a professional massage. If you have the resources, sample various kinds of massage – Swedish, Japanese shiatsu or Thai – and see what appeals to you. If you want to save your money, get a book on massage, read it with a family member or friend and practise on each other.

Besides feeling wonderful, massage makes a great health practice. It relieves stress and insomnia, reduces muscle aches, improves the circulation of blood and lymph, and boosts skin tone and texture. It can also balance your organ systems and your chi, or energy.

Heal your grief

Grief isn't all tears.
Patti Smith, rock musician (b. 1946)

Grief is a combination of sorrow, anger, confusion, disbelief and despair. It's not so much an experience as a process. Sooner or later, each of us finds our own journey through this inevitable aspect of life. You can experience grief for a variety of reasons: because of the death of a family member, partner or friend, or because of the ending of a relationship. You may also feel grief at losing a job you love, your long-time home or even your health.

   If you've experienced a loss, recently or in the past, it's important to get help – from a friend, a minister, a therapist or a support group. Give yourself time to fully process the range of feelings you're going through. Be patient with yourself. Heal your grief in order to face your future with hope and joy.

Explore herbal remedies

The first herbal guide dates back five thousand years, to the Sumerians, who used herbs such as caraway and thyme for healing.
Earl Mindell, author of *Earl Mindell's New Herb Bible*

Herbs have been used by all cultures for millennia for healing and disease prevention. Overall they're safer than synthetic drugs, but they're potent medicine and should be used responsibly. All you need is a little information and common sense.

Read up on any herb that you are considering taking. Stick to the recommended dosage, and watch for allergic reactions or interactions with other herbs and drugs. Used carefully, herbs offer inexpensive and effective remedies for many everyday illnesses, such as the common cold or flu.

Own your shadow

When the blackest aspects of the shadow, the most negative features of one's life and fate, are seen in relation to one's total life destiny, they change their character. They become acceptable and a meaningful part of the whole.

Edward Edinger, Jungian analyst (1922–98)

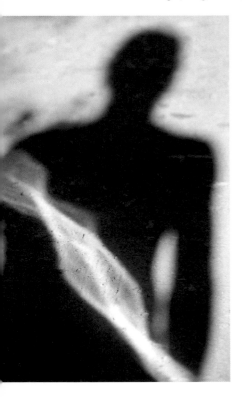

If you want to live a more spiritual life, examine your own shadow – those parts of you that you have trouble owning. Your shadow could be your anger, your wish to control, your greed – anything that you find difficult to admit.

When you do bring these aspects of yourself to light, and fully own them, you'll feel more whole and self-accepting. You'll stop unconsciously projecting your negative aspects onto others, and you'll turn your shadow aspects into energy for positive change.

Stop smoking

Quitting smoking greatly reduces serious risk to your health.

US Surgeon General's warning on cigarette packets

It's not news to anyone that smoking is one of the worst things you can do for your health. Unfortunately, smoking is one of the most difficult addictions to overcome.

If you decide to quit, don't do it alone. See your doctor and explore prescriptions to help you withdraw. Start exercising and breathing more deeply. Stay away from situations where people smoke, such as bars or other social gatherings. Join a support group, and choose a buddy you can call when temptation threatens to get the better of you. Giving up smoking is one of the best things you can do for your health, your longevity and your wallet.

Prevent accidents

The simple fact is that there are many more accidents and deaths in the home than on the roads.

UK government website on home safety

Accidents complicate your life, endanger your health and cost a great deal of money. Simplify and protect your life by doing what you can to avoid accidents.

Keep your electrical wiring in good condition; secure carpets that slip; put non-slip mats in the shower; and repair broken furniture and appliances. Keep your car well maintained, have the tyres properly inflated and drive safely. Make sure that your stairs, walkways, porches and halls are well lit and free of clutter. Lock up cleaning supplies and other potential poisons. Install smoke detectors around your home. A little prevention will save you and your family from a serious accident.

Be your authentic self

No person can wear one face to him or herself, and another to the
multitude, without finally getting bewildered as to which may be true.
Nathaniel Hawthorne, author (1804–64)

Finding and being your authentic self requires a sustained inward
journey. It also takes courage and self-love on your part.

By honestly saying what you feel and think, by behaving in the way
that makes you feel most comfortable, by doing what feels right, you
simplify your life. You'll no longer have the stress and confusion of
wearing two faces. Regardless of the response of others, you'll be more
comfortable in your own skin. You'll find yourself more giving, and more
accepting of others.

Examine saving and hoarding

People unconsciously keep clutter in order to suppress their aliveness. They may want to change and improve their lives, but their subconscious minds are afraid to journey into the unknown.

Karen Kingston, author of *Creating Sacred Space with Feng Shui*

If you have a problem with clutter, you may have a deeper underlying problem: you may be compulsively saving and hoarding. You may have fears of not having enough, or anxiety about abandonment. Or you may feel that you need clutter as a kind of insulation, for protection.

If your clutter problem is over-the-top – that is, if it's beyond simply having too much stuff – get professional help. Sort out any emotional issues. When you feel safe, get friends to help you clean out your clutter and excess possessions.

Eat more vegetables

Numerous research studies and reviews have found that diets rich in fruits and vegetables are associated with reduced risks for chronic diseases and many types of cancer.

US Centers for Disease Control and Prevention

When you're on the go, and you eat on the run, it's easy to skip your vegetables. But you may have forgotten how healthful, delicious and interesting they can be.

Get a good cookbook and experiment with vegetables you don't normally cook. You're probably familiar with broccoli, romaine lettuce and cauliflower, but what about rapini, kolhrabi and bitter melon? Try vegetables as a main course, such as aubergine Parmesan or a hearty vegetable bean soup, with a green salad and wholegrain bread. Try to eat five to ten servings of fruit and vegetables a day.

Don't lie with your silence

Lying is done with words and also with silence.

Adrienne Rich, poet (b. 1929)

Lying is not so easy to define. There are little white lies, big whoppers, lies of exaggeration and inflation, and partial lies that hold back significant pieces of information. Lies of silence, however, are a little harder to define.

If you're in a group and you withhold information crucial to your group decision-making process, are you lying? If you remain quiet when your input could save someone from being wrongly fired, are you lying? If you don't answer when your lover asks if you've cheated on them, are you lying? Try not to use silence as a mask for dishonesty.

Fly prayer flags

Although it isn't necessary to know the meaning of prayer flags when you offer them, you will gain benefit through developing faith and trust in them.

Tai Situpa Rinpoche, lama (b. 1954)

Tibetan Buddhists fly prayer flags as part of their spiritual practice. Prayers and images are printed on a cloth, sewn on a string and hung where they can blow in the wind. The air carries the blessing of the prayers printed on the flags, so the wind becomes blessed. Whatever, and whomever, is touched by that wind receives the blessings.

Prayer flags are offered to increase spirit, success, long life, merit and luck. You can buy Tibetan prayer flags on the Web or at a shop in your area that sells Buddhist goods. You don't have to be Buddhist to benefit from flying prayer flags.

Trust yourself

Trust your instinct to the end, though you can render no reason.
Ralph Waldo Emerson, author and poet (1803–82)

Learn to trust in your own values when you are making decisions and determining what's right for you. When you feel doubt and fear rising over your choices, that's the time to dig deep and ask yourself what you truly feel, and what matters most to you. Examine why the doubt emerged. External pressures, and other people's opinions, can easily undermine your self-confidence in your direction and goals. Work on trusting yourself by checking in with yourself on a daily basis. Stay tuned to your inner compass and feel free to adjust your course if necessary.

Think beyond the traditional church

Everyone needs a faith, a commitment, that is congruent with her or his reason and knowledge, and it must be personal.
Joseph S. Willis, author of *Finding Faith in the Face of Doubt*

You may want a spiritual life, but the traditional church or churches you've attended may not meet your needs. You may have doubts and disappointments and not know where to turn. Instead of just giving up, and denying your spiritual needs, explore alternative traditions.

Learn about the variety of Buddhist paths, such as Tibetan, Zen or Thai path. Explore the Indian Hindu faith or British Wiccan traditions, both of which have a thriving presence outside their native lands. Try alternative Christian denominations. Or create your own unique spiritual practice. Don't give up on finding the path that's right for you.

Write to heal

This writing is for you and you alone. It is for your heart and your health.
Use it only for this journey. It is not meant to be revealed.
Susan Zimmermann, author of *Writing to Heal the Soul*

Painful emotional baggage complicates your life and often leads to addictions or other avoidance behaviour. A therapist can be your best ally, but writing comes a close second and has considerable healing potential.

Buy a special journal and then commit yourself to writing every morning about what has happened to you. Pour your heart into your words. Don't hold anything back. Describe your feelings in detail, and request help from God or a higher power to heal your emotional and psychological wounds.

Organize your life

It's bad. I really need to take control.
Katie Holmes, actress (b. 1978)

You'll get a huge boost in simplifying your life just by getting organized. You waste time and create stress by chasing after misplaced papers and objects. If you can manage the details of your life, you'll free up more time for simply having fun.

Work with one room at a time. Assuming that you've cleared out everything that isn't useful, find the best method of organization for that room. If it's your home office, develop a filing system that works for you. If it's the kitchen, organize your pots and utensils so that they're easy to access — hang them on the wall, if necessary. Get a bulletin board for family use, to keep track of appointments and events. Make a set of hooks for everyone's keys.

Make peace with your parents

Don't hold your parents up to contempt. After all, you are their child, and it is just possible that you may take after them.
Evelyn Waugh, novelist (1903–66)

Unresolved issues with your parents may be preventing you from enjoying life. In order to heal your past, you may need to have a conversation in the present with your parents about past hurts, or misunderstandings that have developed in your adult years.

If you have the courage to talk to your parents openly, you may learn as much about them as they will about you. Whatever happened in your past, try to let go of anger and guilt and create a healthy relationship in the present.

Go on a personal retreat

Always keep a place to which you can retreat.
Chinese proverb

You may be used to going on holiday with friends or family, but this year consider going on a personal retreat instead. Use the time to reconnect with yourself spiritually, to plan for your future or just to think about your life and put it in perspective.

Check on the Web for retreat facilities, or rent a simple cabin somewhere that suits you. Bring books for inspirational reading, and a journal for writing in. You can either go on a short weekend retreat or have a longer sojourn — pick whatever length of time you feel you can handle on your own. Try not to contact other people, but simply to stay in your own company and see what emerges.

Embrace uncertainty

The only thing that makes life possible is permanent, intolerable uncertainty; not knowing what comes next.
Ursula K. Le Guin, author (b. 1929)

Since 9/11 and the attack on the World Trade Center in New York, life feels more uncertain than ever. Economies around the world are struggling. As a result, you may recently have lost your job. Or, because of stress, you may have alienated a lover or friend. You will find that, as hard as you try to nail things down, life has a way of pulling the rug out from underneath you.

You can't prevent uncertainty, as it is the nature of life, but you can learn how to handle it better. Much of our difficulty with uncertainty comes from fighting it. To lessen your stress and fear, fully accept that you don't know what's going to happen next. Don't drain your energy in denial or resisting reality. Learn to relax in the face of the unknown.

Learn about your chakras

By examining your relationship to the different powers and sacred truths inherent in each chakra, you can learn more about where you need to focus your attention and clear out energy blockages.

Carolyn Myss, author of *Carolyn Myss's Journal of Inner Dialogue*

Chakra is a Sanskrit word that means 'wheel'. According to ancient knowledge, we have seven chakras, or energy centres, in our body. The three lower chakras are associated with primary needs, such as survival, money and procreation. The four higher chakras are associated with love, communication, knowledge and wisdom. Your chakras can easily become blocked through stress, or negative thinking, and your symptoms may manifest as physical ailments. For example, if you are having trouble expressing yourself, you might have problems with your throat chakra, which could manifest as thyroid problems.

By learning about your chakras, you can understand how best to keep your energy flowing freely and your chakras unblocked.

Eat good carbohydrates

In theory, at least, low-carb eating is indeed suitable for everyone, because it's the diet the first humans ate, before we left the forest and moved up the evolutionary ladder to the Industrial Revolution – and sugar.

Fran McCullough, author of *Living Low-Carb*

Our obesity epidemic is a clearly a result of over-eating. However, recent research has shifted the blame from eating too much fat to eating too much sugar and white flour. White-flour products (such as pasta, bread, biscuits, crackers and cakes), plus lots of refined sugar, really put on the weight. And they're causing an alarming rise in diabetes and heart disease.

If you eat a lot of starchy carbohydrates, limit yourself to small amounts of wholegrain breads, cereals and pastas. Choose fruit and vegetables that contain lower amounts of sugar and lots of fibre. And avoid refined sugar.

Follow your conscience

We all struggle at times to know what to do to seek and abide by our conscience. The outcome of these struggles affects the course of your life, and the lives around you.

Bill Shore, author of *The Light of Conscience*

Bill Shore is the founder of Share Our Strength, an American non-profit-making organization that has raised more than $100 million (£55 million) to support anti-hunger and anti-poverty organizations worldwide. Share Our Strength has mobilized tens of thousands of individuals to contribute their talents towards anti-poverty efforts.

Consider what you can do to help end hunger and poverty in your town, or in the world at large. Any contribution of your time and effort – however small or brief – will help. When you respond to injustice, you act in harmony with your conscience, and in so doing you may change your life.

Avoid the two-income trap

In a world in which families on television never worry about money, it is hard to grasp the breadth or depth of financial distress sweeping through ordinary suburbs, small towns and nice city neighbourhoods.
Elizabeth Warren and Amelia Warren Tyagi, authors of *The Two-Income Trap*

Middle-class families are frequently in financial trouble today, even though both adults are working. They're taking on big mortgages because they want their kids to go to the best schools. Good schools are found in more affluent neighbourhoods. Unfortunately, banks are all too willing to lend more than the family can really afford. Car loans and credit cards are easily available, and provide a further invitation to go deeper into debt.

If you're in a 'two-income trap', take a good look at your finances and consider moving to a smaller, less expensive home.

Use up your leftovers

*The most remarkable thing about my mother is that for thirty years
she served the family nothing but leftovers. The original meal has
never been found.*

Calvin Trillin, essayist (b. 1935)

What do you do with the leftover ingredients from making a recipe, or
with the leftovers from dinner? You may have good intentions and
dutifully save them, but in a few days they may find their way into your
rubbish bin. You then end up not only losing the food, but losing your
hard-earned money as well.

Your problem may be that you just don't know how to use that
leftover rice, that half cup of green beans or the rest of the tomato
paste. Try reading a cookbook on using up leftovers (ideally one that
lists foods by name, and then suggests recipes for their use) for ideas
about how to utilize leftovers in creative ways.

Discover your sacred contract

You promise to do certain things for yourself, for others and for divine purposes.

Caroline Myss, author of *Sacred Contracts*

Caroline Myss writes that, before we're born, we each agree to the terms of a 'sacred contract'. She feels this is true whether you believe in reincarnation, a single lifetime, an afterlife – or none of these.

As an experiment, imagine that you agreed to a sacred contract before you entered this life. How does this alter the way you see your life to date? If something painful happened to you in the past, instead of thinking of yourself as a victim, consider that it may have been part of your contract. Perhaps you had something to learn, or you needed this event to clear negative karma. What do you think you agreed to do with your life? Are you fulfilling your promise?

Keep a coin jar

A penny saved is a penny earned.

Anonymous

One of the best ways to save money is by keeping a coin jar. A large glass jar works well, and allows you to watch your savings increase.

Every evening empty your pockets or your purse of loose change and put it in the jar. Refrain from removing any coins until the jar is full. When it's full to the brim, take it to the bank and deposit the coins in your savings account. Keep track of what you accumulate and you'll be amazed at the amount of money you will save over a period of a year. If you want a bigger nest egg, start saving your small banknotes as well.

Get enough sleep

In 1910 the average adult was still sleeping nine to ten hours a night.
T. S. Wiley, author of *Lights Out: Sleep, Sugar and Survival*

Up until 80 years ago humans tended to get more sleep – going to bed early and getting up with the sun. Not only do we get less sleep now than we need, but we have lost our connection to the rhythms of nature and the important function of natural light in regulating our hormones.

On average, how many hours a night do you sleep? Do you wake up feeling rested? If you can get by on six hours' sleep, you may feel efficient, but this shortage could be taking a toll on your long-term health. Try going to bed at 9 p.m. and waking up at 6 a.m. Do this for a week and note how you feel.

Buy secondhand items

Diligence is the basis of wealth, and thrift the source of riches.
Chinese proverb

Garage sales, charity shops, flea markets and Internet auction sites all offer a fun way to cut your expenses on necessities and buy luxuries you thought you couldn't afford. If you buy secondhand items, you can have the thrill of the treasure hunt as well as the satisfaction of a basic good deal. Clothes, furniture, books, toys, tools – the choices are endless.

Granted, you have to be a little savvy. Know the purchase price of the item new and what it goes for secondhand. And don't forget to bargain. Who knows? You could end up with a missing masterpiece by Monet, or just a really great deal on clothes for your kids. If you let go of the advertising hype that says you must always buy the newest and best, you can live very well on very little.

Bake your own bread

The very best way to learn to make bread is to bake often, alongside someone who is really good at it.

Bronwen Godfrey, author of *The Laurel's Kitchen Bread Book*

There's nothing more heavenly than the smell of freshly baked bread – except, perhaps, eating a slice of warm, just-cooked bread slathered with butter.

You don't need to bake bread; good bread is available at your local bakery. But if you want to slow down the pace of your life, and enjoy the sensuous pleasure of working with dough, you might give bread-baking a try. Find someone who knows what they're doing and ask for a lesson. Bake your own wholegrain loaves using organic ingredients. And then get ready to treat yourself and your family to low-cost nirvana.

Throw out mail-order catalogues

Discontentment is an illness that infects many people everyday. Look around your life and see where the germs of discontent are breeding.
Deborah Taylor-Hough, author of *Frugal Living for Dummies*

Slick, four-colour mail-order catalogues breed discontentment. It's easy to get emotionally hooked by those gorgeously photographed items you may want, but don't need – and probably can't afford.

Unfortunately, if you've subscribed to one company's catalogues in the past, you may end up being deluged by others, whose companies have purchased a mailing list from the first. If that's the case, get in the habit of throwing the catalogues in the bin when they arrive with your post, without even peeking at their contents. And research sites online where you can sign up to keep junk mail out of your home.

Learn simplicity from others

Finding out who we really are and what we truly want is perhaps best discovered by learning about others who are in the process of doing the same.

Linda Breen Pierce, author of *Choosing Simplicity*

In her book, Linda Breen Pierce reports on her three-year study of 211 people who simplified their lives. Their experiences will give you the courage to move forward in your own quest for simplicity.

Not everyone chooses to simplify their lives in the same way, or starts from the same place, or has the same goals. It's important to find role-models that reflect your own particular situation. Reading about other people's experiences is a great way to get ideas for your own life, as well as to avoid the pitfalls they encountered along the way.

Patronize local farmers' markets

At the farmer's market, freshness is judged by hours, not days. It's a beautiful, sensual experience to go to the market.
Alice L. Waters, food activist and author of *Chez Panisse Café Cookbook*

You may shop at your local supermarket, where you buy produce sealed in shrink-wrapped packages. You don't know the origin of what you buy, and it may well be shipped in from other countries.

For a more sensuous and connected experience, try shopping at your local farmers' market, where the produce is amazingly fresh – just hours from being picked. Enjoy talking with the farmer who grew the gorgeous tomatoes, lettuce or asparagus arranged in front of you. In this way you'll develop a relationship with the earth, with your food and with the people who grow it for you.

Let humour soften your journey

A person without a sense of humour is like a wagon without springs. It's jolted by every pebble on the road.

Henry Ward Beecher, clergyman (1813–87)

The road to a simpler and more spiritual life is not without its potholes. After all, you're making big changes and, unfortunately, they don't always work out.

Your family may mutiny after the third day of 'bean ragout' and head for the nearest fast-food restaurant. That used car you bought to save money may need a new transmission. Or you may find out that you really miss shopping and sneak off to shop. At the spiritual end, you may find that you need a holiday from your higher power.

If some things don't work out, don't take them too seriously or lose heart. Instead, have a good laugh – and try a different bean dish.

Find your true passion

Your true passion should feel like breathing; it's that natural.
Oprah Winfrey, talkshow host (b. 1954)

Look for your passion in unlikely places. Do you love beautiful fabric? Do you enjoy museums and art? Are you the one who livens up the party with your sense of humour? You may have buried your passions in a nine-to-five job, and are discounting your interest in fabric, art or humour as being irrelevant to your life.

For one month keep a note of everything that really excites you – no matter how impractical, insignificant or even grand it seems. This list is a key to your passion: the things that light you up and make you forget to eat. Then begin to honour your passions and bring them to the centre of your life.

Cook ahead

Nothing unravels the seams of quality family time faster than having nothing on hand for dinner.

Mary Beth Lagerborg and Mimi Wilson, authors of *Once-a-Month Cooking*

The best way to save on your food bills is to forget restaurants, and cook and eat at home. Yet, when you come home from work feeling tired and hungry, cooking a meal is the last thing you want to do.

Try combining the cost-effectiveness of cooking from scratch with the convenience of having instant home-cooked meals. Once a month spend a day cooking, packaging and freezing main dishes for the next 30 days. When you get home from work, simply add some steamed vegetables or a green salad and you'll be eating a great, healthy and delicious meal in no time. If you want to invite last-minute guests – no problem!

Ask questions

Sometimes questions are more important than answers.
Nancy Willard, poet and novelist (b. 1936)

If you want to save money by living in a smaller house, ask yourself
what the minimum amount of space should be. Then ask yourself how
you will feel living in a small house. If your answer is scared or unhappy,
ask yourself why you are anticipating these feelings. You may discover
that a small house reminds you of feeling cramped and lacking in
privacy when you were young.

This might bring up insights about your family, and how you've
distanced yourself from them by living in a large house beyond your
means. In fact, you may discover that you really want a cosier, more
intimate home, but that old pain from the past has stood in your way.
Keep asking questions as a means to sort out your life.

Visit a wilderness area

The clearest way into the Universe is through a forest wilderness.
John Muir, naturalist (1838–1914)

It's great to visit nature in your garden, or in your local park, but it's more exciting and humbling to visit nature in a forest or wilderness area.

Visit a wilderness area close to you, if there is one; or, if you have the option of travel, choose one somewhere in the world that sparks your imagination. Go alone and intentionally set your mind on experiencing what the forest and wilderness can teach you. Open yourself to the awesome majesty of nature unspoiled by human endeavours. Sit quietly and meditate on your place in the universe, and your destiny here on Earth.

Break old patterns

When patterns are broken, new worlds emerge.
Tuli Kupferberg, member of Sixties rock band, The Fugs (b. 1924)

Change is difficult and unruly. If you're trying to simplify your life, at times you may feel as if you're destroying more than you're creating. But, if your life isn't working because of over-spending, materialism, lack of spiritual direction and unfulfilling work, then breaking your old patterns of behaviour can open the door to allow a new and better life to emerge.

For example, if you're used to shopping in order to deal with depression, stop shopping and face your pain. If breaking your old patterns is painful, have faith in yourself. Once old, negative patterns are broken, you'll open yourself up to a new and more positive life.

Serve others

Service to others is the rent you pay for your room here on Earth.
Muhammad Ali, boxing champion (b. 1942)

In the Buddhist tradition, a bodhisattva is a person who devotes his or her life to helping others, and relieving their pain and suffering.

It's important to help yourself, and relieve your own pain and suffering, by creating a more sane and balanced life. But it's also important to help others. We're here on Earth both to develop ourselves and to serve others – be they our family, friends, colleagues, church members, fellow citizens of our town and country, or the downtrodden and suffering of the world. Serve others as much as you can in order to create a happier life for yourself.

Resist impulse-buying

If shoppers suddenly ceased to buy on impulse, believe me, our entire economy would collapse.
Paco Underhill, author of *Why We Buy*

The best way to avoid impulse-buying is to make a list before you go shopping, and only shop for specific items. You probably already create grocery lists, but the hard part is disciplining yourself to stick to them. Resist that magazine and chocolate bar at the checkout, and even though they look mouthwateringly delicious don't buy those expensive, imported strawberries in the middle of winter.

The same goes for any type of shopping you may do. If you want to buy a pair of jeans and a T-shirt, stick to your mental list when you go to the shopping centre. Make a beeline for the items you want, buy them and leave. Don't browse among the sale racks as an excuse to purchase something you don't really need.

Learn to drum

The return of the drum into our culture is not yet recognized by the scientific community, but droves of ordinary people are being captivated by its sound, power and magic.

Layne Redmond, author of *When the Drummers Were Women*

Drumming is a fantastic way to reduce stress, connect with your body and connect with other people.

The drum, an ancient instrument, has been used for sacred rituals, and social pleasure, throughout history. Drums echo the rhythms of time, nature and the universe. And you don't have to have any musical experience to learn drumming.

Check out your local area for drum classes or drum circles. Some circles are free for anyone to join. And if you don't own a drum you can usually borrow one.

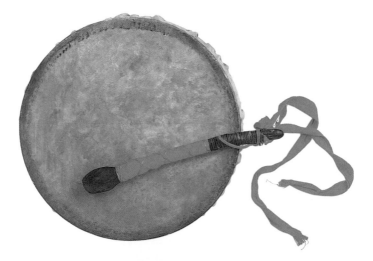

Examine sacred sexuality

If anything is sacred, the human body is sacred.
Walt Whitman, poet (1819–92)

Sex can be banal or sacred. It's all a matter of how you approach it, and how you regard yourself and your partner.

All the great world religions have honoured sexuality, regardless of how repressive their contemporary churches may be. Ask yourself if you have any negative feelings about your body or your sexuality. If you do, work on accepting your body as beautiful and sacred, and on accepting sex as a positive and wholesome activity. Explore sex as a spiritual practice though reading, and sharing ideas with other like-minded people. Allow your sexuality to deepen your understanding of yourself, your partner and the nature of reality. Honour your partner as another sacred being. Together try to use your sexuality to enhance your understanding of divine love.

Be kind to your spine

There is not a nerve in our organism that is not, somehow, dependent on the integral functioning of the spinal cord and consequently the vertebral column.

Vanda Scaravelli, author of *Awakening the Spine*

To have a healthy body you need to have a flexible spine. To have a flexible spine, you need to have strong core muscles – the muscles in your back, abdomen, hips and pelvis. These muscles support and protect the internal organs as well as your spine.

Yoga, or other short exercise programmes, are excellent practices for developing your core muscles. If you have a strong torso, you will be able to handle the physical demands of daily life more easily, and you will rest better at night. So be kind to your spine and give it the support it requires.

Expect your needs to be met

*Expect your every need to be met. Expect the answer to every problem,
expect abundance on every level ...*

**Eileen Caddy, co-founder of the Findhorn Community, Scotland, and author
of *The Dawn of Change***

Your mind is so powerful – what you think shapes your reality. If you're
wanting something to happen, if you're thinking of something you need
and want, then the way you frame your thoughts about those wants will
greatly determine how (or even if) they manifest in your life.

Think of something you want. In expressing your desire, intend that
receiving this thing, or situation, or quality, will not only be for your
benefit but for the benefit of all. Imagine that what you desire has
already been fulfilled. If you expect your dreams to be fulfilled, they have
a greater chance of manifesting.

Don't lose the things that money can't buy

It's good to have money and the things that money can buy, but it's good, too, to check up once in a while and make sure that you haven't lost the things that money can't buy.

George Horace Lorimer, editor-in-chief of Indianapolis's *Saturday Evening Post* **(1868–1937)**

Make a list of the things you feel money can't buy. Your list might include: waking up next to your spouse in the morning; having someone make you chicken soup when you're feeling sick; being listened to and understood when you're distraught; loving your work; watching a horse gallop in a field; smelling the earth after a spring rain shower; or just simple joy at being alive.

When you feel overwhelmed with money problems, take the time to remember the things on your list.

Grow through challenges

Challenges make you discover things about yourself that you never really knew. They're what make the instrument stretch — what make you go beyond the norm.
Cicely Tyson, actress (b. 1933)

Challenges are situations that require the full use of your abilities, energy and resources. By having the courage to take on challenges as they present themselves, you'll have the opportunity to learn about yourself, and possibly to discover hidden strengths and talents that you didn't even know you had.

Challenges can be stressful, but stress is not always a negative factor. When you face a challenge — a health crisis, a sudden divorce or a new, demanding job — you have the chance to grow as a human being.

Focus on your character

Fame is a vapour, popularity an accident, and riches take wings. Only one thing endures and that is character.

Horace Greeley, newspaper editor and politician (1811–72)

Money and fame are fleeting, but what lasts is your character – your moral and ethical strength, and your integrity as a person.

We would all like to be admired, and to have a lot of money. It's easy to justify any actions that might deliver such things. Would you take advantage of someone if it guaranteed you a huge windfall? Have you ever found yourself undermining someone else in order to put yourself forward? In order to avoid the trap of fame and riches, meditate on their fleeting quality. Then spend time defining your own morality and ethics. Strive to preserve your character above all else.

Appreciate librarians

I have a real soft spot in my heart for librarians and people who care about books.

Ann Richards, former governor of Texas (b. 1933)

Libraries are the heart of a free society, and librarians are their unsung caretakers. They work quietly, behind the scenes, to keep a treasure trove of books, and other materials – music, videos and DVDs, newspapers and magazines – organized, maintained and available for your use. They work with architects to design library facilities; they review and order new materials; they teach you how to research subjects, and provide you with suggestions for your reading pleasure. They love and cherish books.

The next time you're at the local library, thank your librarian for the hard work he or she does for you and your community.

Preserve and maintain your energy

The difference between one person and another is not mere ability, it is energy.

Thomas Arnold, educationalist (1795–1842)

Your energy is your life force. It's also called chi or prana in Eastern cultures. If you don't eat well, get enough sleep or exercise and keep a positive state of mind, you reduce your energy and injure your life force. No matter how brilliant and talented you are, you will not be at your best.

Notice how you feel around someone who exudes a positive life force, compared with someone who seems stressed, overweight and puffy from lack of sleep or from eating the wrong foods. Vow to maintain, preserve and enhance your energy through a combination of positive thinking, meditation and physical care.

Read deeply

Anyone who can read, can learn to read deeply, and thus live more fully.
Norman Cousins, editor and essayist (1912–90)

There are many ways to read a book. Since reading takes time, try to bring your best self to the task.

First of all, be choosy about what you read. Read fiction and non-fiction that enhances your life, that teaches you something new, or that inspires, consoles or encourages you to be a better person. Bring your questioning mind, your ability to reason, your capacity to study and learn, your compassion and your empathy to any book that you read. Be willing to be moved emotionally and spiritually, but also be prepared to put the book down and move on, if it isn't really contributing to your life.

Live a high, simple and useful life

There is no power on earth that can neutralize the influence of a high, simple and useful life.

Booker T. Washington, founder of Tuskegee University, Alabama (1856–1915)

How you choose to live your life is not just a personal matter. Your choices affect you, your family, your community, your country and the wider world. If you live a positive and useful life, guided by a well thought-out set of values and goals, no one can change, dilute or make irrelevant your positive contribution to the universe.

You don't have to make a big splash in life, be famous or perform 'great' public acts to have a positive influence on the world. Your decision to live a simpler and more spiritual life will not only help you, but will assist the entire world to move in a positive direction.

Use your power and talents

True happiness involves the full use of one's power and talents.
John W. Gardner, US Secretary of Health, Education and Welfare
(1912–2002)

If you are less than you can be, it will nag at you. Perhaps you know
that you should work harder, but you have a tendency to be lazy. Or you
are an extraordinary cook, but you choose just to heat up something in
the microwave. On a grander scale, maybe you know you should be
running your own company, running for political office or conducting a
symphony, but you're too afraid to try.

It's important to wake up in the morning and live your day using your
powers and talents to the full. The world needs both of these attributes.
You need to develop and use them for your own happiness.

Start a revolution of the heart

The greatest challenge of the day is: how to bring about a revolution of the heart.

Dorothy Day, founder of the Catholic Worker movement (1897–1980)

Money and power are prime motivators in our contemporary cultures. What would our world be like if we put our heart first? What if all our actions were guided by love and compassion, rather than by greed, fear and the desire for power?

When you lead from the heart, your motivation for whatever you do is to create true happiness, and to relieve every kind of suffering – mental, emotional, spiritual and physical. The way you change the world is through one heart at a time. Make your heart the first to change. Then get others to join your revolution of the heart.

Readjust when necessary

Readjusting is a painful process, but most of us need it at one time or another.

Arthur Christopher Benson, author and educationalist (1862–1925)

If your relationship is no longer serving either of you, if your work is unfulfilling, if where you live feels oppressive, if the plans you carefully made in the past are not panning out – then it's time to readjust.

Readjusting can be painful, because you have to let go: of ideas that are no longer viable, of beliefs that are clearly false, of people you loved who are now gone, of attitudes that are no longer serving you. Accept that life requires readjustment on an ongoing basis, and you will avoid stagnation and learn to navigate the process with less stress and more grace.

Vote

Voting is a civic sacrament.

Theodore M. Hesburgh, Catholic priest and past president of Notre Dame University, Indiana (b. 1917)

It's easy not to vote: voting takes time; the ballot may be confusing; you may not know much about the candidates who are running for office; or you may have forgotten to register since you moved to a new location.

Free societies, in which the people have a voice in how their government is run, are precious. Consider that there are many countries in the world where democracy is not yet functioning or viable. The next time you think that voting just is not worth it, or you feel jaded and disillusioned, remember that your voice is important. By using it, you have the power to create a more compassionate and effective government – for yourself, and for everyone else in your country.

Commit to reaching your goals

Unless commitment is made, there are promises and hopes, but no plans.
Peter F. Drucker, author and business consultant (b. 1909)

Why do many of your New Year's resolutions fail? Probably because, deep down, you didn't really commit to them. Having a clear intention, and committing yourself to achieving whatever it is that you want to achieve, is an engine that powers accomplishment of all kinds. Your unconditional commitment can move mountains.

Why then is it difficult to make commitments? You may fear having to change, or being fully responsible for your life. Or perhaps you fear closing the door on other options. Examine why you avoid commitment and fail to achieve your goals. Work to let go of those beliefs and behaviour.

Make life sweet

Life is short, and it is up to you to make it sweet.
Sarah Louise Delany, educationalist (1889–1999)

If you experience someone as 'sweet', you may find him or her to be gentle, kind, light-hearted, tender, easy to be with, open-hearted and youthful. If you want to make life sweet for yourself, bring those qualities into your own life.

Live at a slower, more human pace. Be tender in your dealings with others. Try to be someone with whom other people are comfortable. Be generous and empathetic. If others are burdened with difficulties, lift their spirits with humour and understanding. Enjoy life's simple pleasures – the sweetness of freshly shelled peas, or the exuberance of daffodils in the spring. And by all means stay young at heart. Sarah Delany, who advocated making life sweet, died at the age of 109.

Keep your appointments

Unfaithfulness in the keeping of an appointment is an act of clear dishonesty. You may as well borrow a person's money as his time.
Horace Mann, educationalist (1796–1859)

If you have a tendency to 'run late', consider how this affects others in your life. When you ask for an appointment with someone – for dinner, a movie or a business meeting – you have asked him or her for a portion of their time and life energy. When you are 10, 15, 20 minutes late, or more, you're effectively borrowing their time, without their permission.

Don't say you're going to be there at 7 p.m. and arrive breathless, full of apologies and excuses, at 7.30. Honour your friends, your loved ones, your business associates and yourself, by keeping your appointments.

Enjoy simple pleasures

I adore simple pleasures. They are the last refuge of the complex.
Oscar Wilde, playwright (1854–1900)

You may have a preconceived idea of what will bring you pleasure, and then pursue whatever it is that you desire. But one key to a happy life is the ability to appreciate simple pleasures as they arise. It might be the sight of yellow daffodils in a white vase, the beauty of red strawberries against a blue bowl, the taste of home-made bread warm from the oven, or seeing the sunrise in the morning. It might be holding your child as he or she sleeps in your arms, the joy of clean sheets or the relaxation of a warm bath.

Rather than seeking pleasure, the trick is to be present, aware and open to the pleasures all around you.

Go fly a kite

Anyone can learn to fly a kite and experience the thrill of playing with the force of the air.

Sarah Kent, author of *The Creative Book of Kites*

The earliest account of kite-flying occurred in China around 500 BCE. Kites are flown in every culture – they're used for science, sport and good old-fashioned fun. We all enjoy watching a kite soaring on a sunny day. But flying one is even more fun. Try kite-flying to entice your kids, and yourself, off the couch and away from the computer or TV screen.

Buy a simple paper kite, or make your own. Use inexpensive materials such as wood, paper, fabric or plastic. Books on kite-making are in every local library. Consider making kites as a special family project, then go to a park or beach on a windy day for picnicking and kite-flying.

Have an open mind

Above all, remember that the most important thing you can take anywhere is not a Gucci bag or French-cut jeans; it's an open mind.
Gail Rubin Bereny, author (b. 1942)

An open mind is a flexible, receptive mind. It's a mind that holds thoughts and beliefs lightly. Having an open mind gives you the opportunity to learn and develop intellectually and spiritually.

If you have an open mind, you will be able to change easily, adjust your thinking and learn things that may even contradict everything you have ever thought before. By having an open mind, you'll have the capacity to grow as a person, be more tolerant of others and be the best you can be in all areas of life. An open mind is like water: it flows easily around obstacles and can take on different forms for different purposes. An open mind is a creative mind.

Use weekends for relaxation

Weekends don't count unless you spend them doing something completely pointless.

Bill Watterson, author of Calvin and Hobbes cartoons (b. 1958)

Weekends were invented by labour unions to give people time off from work, to rest and spend time with their families. But how often are your weekends as frenetic as your work week – filled with projects, errands or various maintenance activities?

You don't have to do something you consider 'pointless', but if that helps you then do so. Make sure you spend at least half a day in conscious relaxation. Go for a walk, sit in your garden with a cool drink and a good book, or just take a nap. Do this for your physical, emotional, psychological and spiritual health.

Use prayer beads

The most compelling reason for using beads in prayer is that they are a physical reminder of the state of divinity we have been born into.

Manuela Dunn-Mascetti, author of *The Prayer Bead Box*

Prayer protects the mind from negativity, awakens innate goodness, serenity and other virtues, and helps access the divine. Almost all religions make use of prayer beads.

The stringing of beads allows the one who is praying to keep count easily of the number of prayers or mantras repeated. As you pray, the prayer beads connect your body with your mind. You can either buy prayer beads or make your own. Try researching the spiritual use and meaning of various beads, and create your own personal rosary or mala.

Be willing to take a leap

You've got to jump off cliffs and build your wings on the way down.
Ray Bradbury, science-fiction writer (b. 1920)

Some people who like extreme sports actually do jump off cliffs.
However, Ray Bradbury is referring to the metaphorical cliffs of life –
those moments when, in order to go forward, you have to take a leap
into the unknown.

It's exciting, scary and exhilarating, and very hard to do. Regardless
of all that, have the courage to try. As you go forward into your new
venture (be it moving to a new location or starting your new novel),
remember that you'll have your fine intelligence, your past life experience
and your best instincts to guide you. If you take the leap, you'll grow
new wings to meet the challenge.

Learn about silence from the Quakers

Quakers believe that only when we have silenced our voices and our souls can we hear the 'still small voice' that dwells within each of us – the voice of God.

Robert Lawrence Smith, author of *The Quaker Book of Wisdom*

Quakers do not have church services. Instead they have prayer meetings where everyone prays together in silence. They sit together on simple benches, 'centre' themselves and wait for God to speak to them directly. If someone is so moved, he or she rises and shares his or her message.

Have your own Quaker prayer meeting at home with loved ones and friends. Sit with them in silence, and centre and open yourself to God or your higher power. Encourage anyone present to share his or her experience of the divine. After an hour, end your prayer meeting by holding hands.

Try folk dancing

When you extend your arm, it doesn't stop at the end of your fingers,
because you're dancing bigger than that; you're dancing spirit.
Judith Jamison, American dancer (b. 1943)

If you're looking for a way to meet people and have a lot of fun, try folk
dancing. Besides being great entertainment, folk dancing is a good way
to learn about the history and spirit of many diverse cultures. Most folk
dances were traditionally performed for seasonal festivals, weddings or
other social occasions. Try contra dance, Balkan dance, ballroom dance,
Cajun dance, Scottish country-dance, English country-dance,
international dance, Israeli dance, clog dance, Zydeco dance and all
other types of traditional dance.

When looking for a folk-dancing group, try local ethnic churches, adult
education programmes or colleges. If you're shy or feel awkward, don't
worry, for you won't have to perform alone. Most groups provide
newcomers with training.

Say yes to life

To say yes, you have to sweat and roll up your sleeves and plunge both hands into life up to the elbows.

Jean Anouilh, playwright (1910–87)

You may be cautious for a reason. Perhaps you've suffered harm in the past, or you've witnessed others take risks and hurt themselves. As a result, you may be fearful of living fully and passionately.

Write down ten ways you may be holding yourself back from life. Your list may include being afraid to express your love to a special person, refusing to say what you really think or feel at work, or not going on that trip to India that you dream about. You may be hiding out at home alone in front of the TV, instead of taking the risk to meet new people. Consider how you can let go of holding back and say 'yes' to life.

Ask only for what people can give

To live happily with other people, ask of them only what they can give.
Tristan Bernard, playwright and novelist (1866–1947)

It's important to ask for what you need in life – from your partner, your children, your friends, your colleagues, your boss. But it's also important to be wise and compassionate in what you ask for.

Learn to accurately assess the capacities and needs of others, before you make a request. If your partner is having an especially stressful time at work, it's probably not the best moment to discuss changes in your love life. If he or she has no desire or ability to be a gourmet cook, don't ask him or her to learn. When you ask things of others, be realistic and sensitive and your relationships will be harmonious.

Explore sacred sound

A tone lies at the foundation of everything in the physical world.
Rudolph Steiner, social philosopher (1861–1925)

You may think of sound as practical (a way to communicate with others, protect yourself, learn or work) or as a source of pleasure (music, singing, the sounds of nature). But you may not think of sound as spiritual or having the capacity to heal.

Researchers are beginning to document the healing role of sound in destroying cancer cells. Individuals interested in the spiritual and healing qualities of sound are getting together to practise toning sacred syllables such as 'Om'. Taoist healing practices encourage the toning of certain vowels combined with the visualization of organ systems. Educate yourself in the use of sacred sound through reference books.

Let your children make their own way

The finest inheritance you can give your children is to allow them to make their own way, completely on their own feet.

Isadora Duncan, dancer (1877–1927)

If you're a parent, you want the best for your children and you have a strong instinct to protect them from harm. But these natural parental instincts can become negative when you over-direct and over-protect. By doing so, you rob your children of the opportunity to develop their own strengths.

When you act on your child's behalf, ask yourself, 'Am I just making myself feel better, or is this really the best action to take for my child? Am I supporting my child in choosing what's best for him or her? Am I facilitating my child in learning what he or she needs to make his or her own choices?'

Love as Christ and Buddha loved

All that is necessary to make this world a better place to live in is to love – to love as Christ loved, as Buddha loved.
Isadora Duncan, dancer (1877–1927)

When you think of love, you may think of romance. Or you may think of love for your nearest and dearest – your family and friends. Wanting to be loved may also come to mind.

There is a larger meaning of love that doesn't discriminate between the lovable and the unlovable, between the worthy and the unworthy, or between the stranger and the friend. Buddha and Christ taught us to love every living being, regardless of who they are or what they mean to you.

Don't expect defeat

We are not interested in the possibilities of defeat. They do not exist.
Queen Victoria, monarch of Great Britain (1819–1901)

If you're expecting defeat, or anticipating failure, you most likely will be defeated or fail. You may feel that anticipating a negative outcome is good protection against the pain of disappointment. Or, by predicting your own defeat, you may give yourself the illusion of control over your future.

Unfortunately, by expecting defeat you're not only inviting it, you're actually creating it. If you're a pessimist by nature, the negative mental images that you habitually entertain, and the scenarios of failure that you rehearse over and over again, will only guarantee future negativity and failure. In other words, if you've applied for a great new job, expect to be hired. Work to create a positive life, through positive mental imagery and visualization.

Be kinder than necessary

Shall we make a new rule of life from tonight: always to try to be a little kinder than is necessary?
Sir James M. Barrie, playwright (1860–1937)

In order to be kinder than necessary, you'll have to spend time observing others and being sensitive to their needs. If you see that the person at the checkout is tired and stressed, help them by bagging your own groceries. Smile at the crabby bank clerk and ask them about their day. Offer to mow your neighbour's lawn when they've been sick. Make a dinner date with a friend who's going through a hard time.

Try to generate positive energy in any situation by thinking of the needs of others and then acting on them. Your efforts to be kind will increase your own happiness.

Celebrate the solstice

Could there be a connection between our ignorance of the seasonal festivals and our loss of relatedness with one another and the Earth?
Richard W. Heinberg, author of *Celebrate the Solstice*

People in traditional cultures were in tune with the rhythms of nature, because their livelihood depended on planting and harvesting at the proper times. The summer and winter solstices – the longest and shortest days of the year – were times of feasting and celebration. Christmas (winter solstice) and Easter (spring equinox) are two obvious modern holidays that coincide with the older tradition.

Try to bring an awareness of the seasons into your life by celebrating the solstices and the spring and autumn equinoxes (the times of equal-length day and night). Four times a year, have friends and family over for feasting, drinking and dancing.

Seek contentment, not luxury

Contentment is natural wealth, luxury is artificial poverty.
Socrates, philosopher (469–399 BCE)

You may think that material wealth is a key ingredient for having a happy and contented life. But contentment is a state of mind and doesn't depend on anything external.

If you're content, you're satisfied with what you have, regardless of how little that is. You have the ability to be relaxed and centred in any situation. You live passionately, express your deepest self and love others – and yourself – unconditionally. You enjoy owning material possessions, but you don't let them own you. Your contentment is your real wealth. Increase your contentment by living in the moment and expressing gratitude for the life you have.

Create your own altar

*A woman's personal altar evokes her particular – her intimate –
relationship to the divine, human and natural realms.*

Kay Turner, author of *Beautiful Necessity*

One way to create sacred space is to make your own altar. Create an
altar with images and sacred objects from your spiritual tradition, or
make one that is a unique expression of your relationship with the
divine. You may also choose to create an altar for other purposes: to
focus on life goals, or to deal with the loss of a loved one.

Try to make an altar with natural objects,
such as stones, feathers, shells and
flowers, to help you stay connected
to the natural rhythms of the
universe. If it suits your needs,
you could create several
altars for different purposes.

Don't whine

Whining is not only graceless, but can be dangerous. It can alert a brute that a victim is in the neighbourhood.

Maya Angelou, poet (b. 1928)

Besides being irritating to others, whining betrays an unhealthy approach to life. When you're whining, you're usually complaining about something, expressing your dissatisfaction with a person or situation and presenting yourself as a victim. When you're in whining mode, you're being manipulative and passive-aggressive, with the intention of getting someone to help or take care of you. Whining is both disempowering and dishonest.

If you're a whiner, begin to take responsibility for what happens to you in life. Empower yourself by owning and dealing with your own problems. Learn to express yourself clearly, honestly and directly.

Practise equanimity

In order to practise loving-kindness and compassion towards all beings you have to be able to focus on them with equal concern, which is why practising equanimity is so important.
Sermey Khensur Lobsand Tharchin, lama (b. 1921)

We usually sort people into three piles – friends, enemies and neutrals. On a more subtle level, you may find yourself feeling one up, or one down, with friends, loved ones or those whom you consider 'difficult'. You may find yourself shifting your relationship with people over time. Your previous 'best friend' may now be your enemy, and your one-time enemy may now be your beloved partner. Try to avoid sorting people into categories, or competing for power.

Practise seeing everyone as being just like yourself – that is, wanting to find happiness and trying to avoid suffering. This is the beginning of compassion.

Clear your space

Before doing any space clearing, it's best to do a thorough house-cleaning, followed by a de-clutter session.
Denise Linn, author of *Space Clearing A–Z*

Your home or office can easily become cluttered and disorganized. Worse, it can become energetically stagnant and polluted.

Clean your space and get rid of clutter. Then, using a stick of incense, go round the entire room (including the corners) and purify the air. Next, go round the room and clap your hands to move any stagnant energy. Be sure to clap in the corners and around furniture.

There are many other space-clearing techniques you can learn. The important thing is to be aware that your working or living space should be cleared of negative and stagnant energy on a regular basis.

Play the hand you're dealt

Life is like a game of cards. The hand you are dealt is determinism; the way you play it is free will.
Jawaharlal Nehru, statesman (1889–1964)

Life is never fair. You may have a physical disability; or your mother may have abandoned you at birth; or you may have lost everything in a natural disaster. On a less dramatic note, you may have a collection of ordinary problems that simply make your life difficult.

Regardless of what life presents – good or bad – the way you respond makes all the difference. Don't waste your time and energy complaining about the hand that's been dealt to you. Instead, bring all your intelligence and capacities to bear in creating the best life you can, now and in the future. Inspire yourself with the life stories of people who have overcome great adversity and triumphed.

Look for God outside the Bible

God writes the gospel not in the Bible alone, but on trees, and flowers, and clouds, and stars.

Martin Luther, religious reformer (1483–1546)

You may find yourself shrinking God down to fit into the confines of your church, or into the pages of a holy book. Perhaps you feel more comfortable with the idea of the divine when you can manage it. But divinity can't be contained, measured or safely compartmentalized. The divine is everywhere. All beings are sacred; and all nature and matter are expressions of the divine mind. Try expanding your notion of God to encompass the entirety of your life, and all reality. Try experiencing every moment as sacred. When you drive to work, appreciate the sacred landscape. When you look into another's face, see God.

Start a women's circle

*The circle is an archetypal form that feels familiar to the psyches of
most women. It's personal and egalitarian.*
Jean Shinoda Bolen, author of *The Millionth Circle*

If you're a woman, consider starting a women's circle. Your circle might
be a support group for working mothers. Or you could start a women's
spirituality circle, exploring the Goddess in her many forms. Or start a
singing and chanting circle, and take turns in leading it.

Get together with a group of women friends and relatives and
discuss what type of circle might best serve everyone. Open your circle
with a statement of intention. When you close your circle, dedicate
the positive energy you shared for the benefit of yourselves and all
other beings.

Act how you'd like to be

Great is the force of memory and imagination, excessive great, O my
God; a large and boundless chamber!
St Augustine, Catholic saint (354–430 CE)

Visualizing, and acting how you would like to be are powerful tools for change. If you want to lose weight, visualize yourself weighing less, and act as if you're already at the weight you desire. If you want to be a more responsible and mature person, act as if you are. If you want to have more wisdom and spiritual development, act as if you already do. If you want to find a kind and loving partner, be a kind and loving person.

Your mind and imagination are powerful tools for change. Use them creatively to accelerate your growth and transformation into the person you would ideally like to be.

Make responsible choices

Choice of attention – to pay attention to this and ignore that – is to the inner life what choice of action is to the outer. In both cases, a person is responsible for his or her choice and must accept the consequences.

W. H. Auden, poet and essayist (1907–73)

You may think of choices as something that you make occasionally throughout your day – what to cook for dinner, what to buy in the sales, what movie to see. But the reality is that you're making choices each and every moment.

The ancient law of karma states that every choice you make – by your thought or actions – has a consequence. The consequences of your choices may present themselves in this life or in future lives. Whether or not you believe in the law of karma, it helps to live by it. By paying attention to your thinking and your actions, you'll make more responsible choices. By making more responsible choices, you'll improve your life and that of those around you.

Don't let facts obscure the truth

There's a world of difference between truth and facts. Facts can obscure truth.

Maya Angelou, poet (b. 1928)

Facts are only part of the truth – they can never be all the truth. The truth is a rich tapestry of nuance, sensations, feelings, agreed-upon facts and interpretations. Don't shove facts forward to screen what really happened.

The fact may be that the law was followed to the letter, but the truth is that a grave injustice may have been done. The fact may be that you were at work on time, but the truth is that you spent half an hour getting coffee and chatting. The fact may be that you attended class, but the truth is that your mind was at the beach.

Work on sharing

Sharing is sometimes more demanding than giving,
Mary Catherine Bateson, writer and cultural anthropologist (b. 1939)

'Plays well with others' is a phrase that often appears on children's school reports. It usually means the child is able to share toys and compromise. What kind of report would you get as an adult?

Sharing requires giving up control, being willing to negotiate, and being flexible and generous. If you're sharing a car with someone, a living space, an office or just cooking a meal together, you'll need to consciously work on the qualities that promote harmonious sharing.

Give up wanting to be in control of the situation. Be open to other ideas and methods. Be creative in how you incorporate the needs of everyone present. Be flexible if plans change. Be generous in contributing your skills and knowledge when collaborating with others.

Let go of ego and desire

People say 'I want peace.' If you remove I (ego), and your want (desire), you are left with peace.
Satya Sai Baba, spiritual teacher (b. 1926)

Your 'I' is a kind of queen bee. The queen is the centre of her hive, and your ego makes you feel that you're the centre of your universe. That continual self-focus/self-absorption not only gets you into trouble by creating negative emotions like hatred and jealousy, but keeps you from developing spiritually. Desire – the continual 'I want' – fuels your queen-bee mind.

Try to lessen your focus on yourself and on your restless, insatiable desires. Do this by thinking of others more than yourself, and by being satisfied with what you have in the moment.

Use your money positively

Money can be translated into the beauty of living, a support in misfortune, an education, or future security. It also can be translated into a source of bitterness.

Sylvia Porter, financial expert and journalist (1913–91)

Money can be used for either positive or negative reasons. It can be a great support, or a source of contention.

Don't let money come between you and your partner. Work out your differences in how you spend, save and give away money. Once you come to an agreement, try to minimize the influence of money on your life. Recognize that it is only one aspect of your wealth, and that 'assets' like love, good health, friends, children, your education and spiritual life are just as important. Use your money to create positive energy in your life.

Love people

I tell you, the more I think, the more I feel that there is nothing more truly artistic than to love people.

Vincent Van Gogh, artist (1853–90)

Van Gogh's conclusion after a life passionately devoted to painting is an extraordinary statement. Love, he says, is the highest artistic expression. Perhaps it's the highest human expression of all.

On our deathbeds we will not be thinking of that new car we bought, or of the size of our bank account, or of our worldly achievements. We will most likely be thinking of love – those whom we have loved, and those who were kind enough to love us. While there's still time, love yourself and everyone you know. Love those you don't know. Love all sentient beings unconditionally.

Explore the divine feminine

Goddess religion was earth-centred, not heaven-centred, of this world, not otherworldly, body-affirming, not body-denying, holistic, not dualistic.
Elinor W. Gadon, author of *The Once and Future Goddess*

At one time, long ago, the divine was female. Goddesses dominated religious life until around 3000 BCE. And, although the divine feminine is no longer ascendant, she is still a part of all Western and Eastern cultures, with the exception of Islam. Consider the passionate devotion to Mary in the Catholic religion, or the reverence shown to the female Buddha Tara in the Tibetan Buddhist tradition. Hindus worship many female deities, as do Native American and African cultures. Meditating on divinity in female form is balancing for both men and women. Research and choose a female emanation of the divine, and meditate on her qualities.

Grace others with your cheerfulness

You find yourself refreshed by the presence of cheerful people. Why not make an honest effort to confer that pleasure on others?

Lydia Marie Child, author and social reformer (1802–80)

There's nothing better than being in the presence of someone with a cheerful heart. You can't help feeling graced by their positive energy. If you're feeling anxious and distressed, a cheerful person can take your mind off your problems and change your perspective, so that you look at things from a more positive point of view.

It's easy to have a long face – there's plenty in life to be upset about. Even so, try to have a cheerful outlook, and be that cheerful person for other people. Not only will you help others, but you'll lift your own mood as well.

Don't confuse moving fast with going somewhere

Moving fast is not the same as going somewhere.
Dr Robert Anthony, author of *Think Big*

You've no doubt seen suited business people, rushing as they walk down a bustling city street, shoulder to shoulder, hurrying to catch their subway or commuter trains. But where is everybody really going? Our culture equates speed with achievement and success. Perhaps we rush because it gives ourselves – or others – the illusion that we're actually accomplishing something.

If you feel caught up in this frenetic pace of life, ask yourself if your rushing is positive or negative. Are you moving towards well thought-out, life-affirming goals? Or are you running to avoid loneliness or intimacy, or to stem your fear of failure? Make sure your lifestyle serves your health, your spirit and your soul.

Heal your broken heart

To love at all is to be vulnerable. Love anything and your heart will certainly be wrung and possibly be broken.
C. S. Lewis, author (1898–1963)

Break-ups are one of the more traumatic experiences of intimate life. Whether you've just divorced your spouse or ended a relationship with your lover, try to process your feelings and get on with your life.

You may feel rejected, or guilty, or even humiliated. If you're having trouble functioning in everyday life, get help. Try meditating on impermanence. Regardless of how much we want to deny it, life is constantly changing. Acknowledge the reality that you, your partner and your relationship are all impermanent. Try to release the other person — and your past — without acrimony, and to focus on enjoying life now.

Make a pilgrimage

Religion points to that area of human experience where in one way or another a person comes upon mystery as a summons to pilgrimage.
Frederick Beuchner, novelist (b. 1926)

No matter what your religion or spiritual practice, there are many sacred sites around the world for you to visit. Instead of travelling purely for pleasure, consider making a pilgrimage to a holy site to increase your knowledge of your tradition, and to grow spiritually.

If you're Catholic, you may want to visit the Vatican or Lourdes. If you're Buddhist, you may want to visit Bodhgaya, or other places in India where the historical Buddha taught. If you're Muslim, you may want to make your pilgrimage to Mecca. If you're Jewish, you may want to visit Jerusalem. If you don't practise any religion, you might still want to make a pilgrimage to any one of the holy sites mentioned above.

Develop your intuition

Intuition, ESP, paranormal intelligence, high sense perception, the third eye, the sixth chakra — whatever you choose to call it — is part of our natural human endowment.

Belleruth Naparstek, author of *Your Sixth Sense*

We live in a literal, linear, materialistic culture. Yet, perhaps because we are so unbalanced, we have an enormous interest in energetic forms of intelligence, such as those noted above.

Some of us have ready access to our intuition. Fortunately, those of us who don't still have the potential to increase our intuitive skills. Using your energetic, non-verbal intelligence enhances your power to learn, make personal and business decisions, take better care of your health and develop spiritually. Look for workshops in your area on developing your intuition, or read books on the subject.

Cook for spiritual nourishment

When things are properly understood, one's whole life is like a ritual or a ceremony.

Chogyam Trungpa, lama (1939–87)

Food is intimately linked with ceremony and ritual throughout all cultures. Special foods accompany changes in the seasons, rites of transition, and religious and secular holidays. Consider Easter eggs and the Christian tradition: seeds, eggs and fruit signify the renewal of life. In Turkey, special honey cakes are prepared for weddings. In Mexico, little skulls made of sugar are prepared for the Day of the Dead.

The eating of sacred food nourishes you emotionally, psychologically and spiritually. It helps you connect with others in your family and community through shared experience. What foods do you prepare on special occasions? If you don't, consider creating special meals to mark specific holidays and festivals. Talk to your family about the significance of the foods you prepare.

Don't confuse love and love addiction

Instead of developing mature intimacy, love addicts seek to enmesh, to merge, to get completely connected to their partners.
Pia Mellody, author of *Facing Love Addiction*

If you obsess about your partner and try to control him or her, or want to be joined at the hip, you might be a love addict. Childhood experiences of abandonment and other traumas may play a part in your problem.

If you're a love addict, you're most often attracted to people who avoid intimacy. By being attracted to those who aren't available, you set the stage for a painful dance of closeness and rejection. If you're a love addict, try to get help from a therapist or a support group.

Consult the *I Ching*

The philosophy unveiled in the I Ching is simple and consistent: if we relate correctly, keeping our self in tune with the Cosmos, all things work out beneficially for all concerned.

Carol K. Anthony, author of *A Guide to the I Ching*

The *I Ching or Book of Changes* is an ancient Chinese divination manual and book of wisdom. It doesn't give you specific answers to your questions, but it does reveal patterns that can help you arrive at the answers you seek.

The answers are given in 64 hexagrams (groups of six lines) made of solid lines (yang) and broken lines (yin). You consult the *I Ching* by tossing three coins six times, to create two six-line hexagrams. Tails equal a value of two, and heads a value of three. Various combinations of coins determine whether the line is yin or yang. After you throw the coins, refer to a book on the *I Ching* for an explanation of the two hexagrams that you tossed.

Consult the *I Ching* for personal growth, to stimulate creativity and for insight in difficult situations.

Invoke Tara, the female Buddha

In true reality, Tara is a great wisdom being, the feminine principle of Buddha.

Gehlek Rimpoche, author of *Good Life, Good Death*

Tara is the best-known and most beloved feminine deity of Buddhism. She vowed to help others, while always remaining in the female form. Her speciality is teaching self-love and compassion for others.

Tara grants healing and longevity, and protects you from fears that manifest as jealousy, pride and obsession. She is the embodiment of enlightened mind in female form. She appears as a white goddess seated on a lotus and moon cushion, is dressed in fine silks and jewels and is radiantly beautiful. Turn to her when life seems overwhelming. Meditate on her qualities and strive to become like her.

Use affirmations

The practice of engaging in affirmations allows us to begin replacing some of our stale, worn-out or negative mind chatter with more positive ideas and concepts.

Shakti Gawain, author of *Create Your Own Affirmations*

Affirmations – or statements of the existence of something – are powerful tools for moving your life in a positive direction. Stating to the universe that what you want to happen has already happened creates the energy for its manifestation.

Ready-made affirmations may not be as effective as writing your own. Write down three affirmations that are specific to you for meeting your goals. Instead of saying, 'I am free of addiction', you might write, 'I am free of my addiction to sugary foods, especially ice cream'. Your mind will help you to achieve your goals if you give it specific suggestions in the form of affirmations. Say your affirmations out loud three times a day.

Explore tai chi

Patience and the curbing of impulsiveness are attained through the study of Tai Chi because we learn to accept our own natural rate of change.
Robert Chuckrow, author of *The Tai Chi Book*

Tai chi is an internal martial art that emphasizes very slow movements, inward focus and health. In China it's not uncommon to see people of all ages practising tai chi together in the park before going to work. You may even see practitioners in their nineties gracefully executing the movements of their form.

Tai chi is great for maintaining flexibility and balance. It's also a good practice for reducing stress. Check out your local area for classes in tai chi. Some schools may require you to have a simple uniform of trousers and a jacket.

Be an optimist

Optimism doesn't wait on facts. It deals with prospects. Pessimism is a waste of time.

Norman Cousins, editor and essayist (1912–90)

Optimists have positive anticipation of the future, regardless of what's happening in the present. They don't dwell on past mistakes or problems. They tend to be healthier, live longer and feel more satisfied with their lives.

According to researcher Martin Seligman, optimists think good things happen because of permanent causes, such as 'I'm smart', and bad things happen because of temporary situations, like 'My boss was in a bad mood'. He also found that optimism is a learned behaviour. So if you're a pessimist there's still hope for you.

Study myths to understand your life

Myths are clues to the spiritual potentialities of the human life.
Joseph Campbell, author and scholar on comparative religion (1904–87)

Myths are stories that speak to you in metaphors. They teach you what it is to be human. Archetypes like 'the hero', 'the magician' or 'the warrior' are the characters in the story. You may recognize the myths retold in plays, movies or novels. The film *Star Wars* is a great hero's tale.

Think of your own life in mythic, archetypal terms. As a hero, what journey are you on? What are you searching for? As a warrior, what hardships are you transcending? As a magician, how are you creatively living your life?

Be willing to try something new

I resist change even as I call for it.
Mason Cooley, American aphorist (b. 1928)

It's easy to get used to doing things in a certain way. You may have specific business practices that worked in the past, and so you resist change out of fear or a habit of being rigid. Your church or social organization may be stuck in a rut, and those in charge may be invested with preventing change in order to keep control. 'We've always done it that way' is a familiar refrain. Or you may personally have some negative habits, such as paying your bills late or drinking too much, but not know how to change.

The answer to all of the above is: be willing to try something new. Be open to doing something different, in your personal, organizational and work life.

Teach your kids origami

A limitless universe of possibilities is concealed in the small — usually about six to a side — square of paper used in folding origami.
Kunihiko Kasahara, author of *Origami for the Connoisseur*

Origami, the Japanese art of paper folding, is a delightful, inexpensive and highly creative craft to teach your children. You may just get hooked on it yourself! All you need is some ordinary paper and some directions to follow.

Check your local library for a book on origami, or find instructions on origami websites. You'll learn how to fold miniature animals, insects, birds, boats, furniture, puzzles, flowers, aeroplanes, boxes and containers. After you've practised on plain white paper, try using coloured or patterned papers appropriate for the project. Some art shops sell papers specifically for origami.

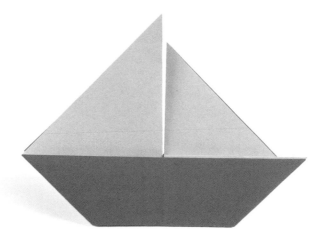

Heal with crystals and gemstones

Crystals heal holistically. That is to say, they work on the physical, emotional, mental and spiritual levels of being. They realign subtle energies and dissolve disease, getting to the root cause.

Judy Hall, author of *The Crystal Bible*

Crystals and gemstones have energetic properties and produce healing vibrations. When placed close to or on your body, they can affect your health in positive ways.

Use the highest-quality gemstones – those that are not dyed or irradiated to enhance their colour. Go to a gem shop and see which stones attract you, or consult a book to choose crystals or gemstones for specific purposes. For instance, diamonds help allergies and other chronic conditions; lapis lazuli relieves migraine and cleanses the immune system; turquoise helps you to assimilate nutrients.

Beware of small expenses

Beware of small expenses; a small leak will sink a great ship.
Benjamin Franklin, statesman and inventor (1706–90)

Small expenditures for parking meters, coffee and soft drinks, newspapers, bus fares, postage stamps, magazines, sweets, or road and bridge tolls can drain your budget. When keeping track of your expenses you may discount these seemingly inconsequential items and not bother to track them. But over time such small expenses add up.

Track these little purchases over a month and see if you can cut down or even eliminate them. Take the money you would have spent and put it in your savings account. After a year, take the money and put it towards a well-earned holiday.

Give yourself away

*I would like to believe when I die that I have given myself away like a
tree that sows seed every spring and never counts the loss, because it
is not loss, it is adding to future life.*

May Sarton, poet and author (1912–95)

It's easy to be caught in a mindset of preservation. You may want to
preserve your health, your youth, your energy, your time, your money or
your skin. This mindset causes you to hold back from life, and perhaps
hold back your gifts from the world.

If you want to give yourself more in love, don't hold back your
feelings. If you have something to express, write the book, paint the
painting or create the music. If you're a scientist, apply for your research
grant. For sure, take care of yourself. But try to spend your life
generously sharing your gifts and talents
with the world, for the benefit of all
beings – present and future.

Assess your emotional intelligence

Emotional life is a domain that, as surely as math or reading, can be handled with greater or lesser skill, and requires its unique set of competencies.

Daniel Goleman, author of *Emotional Intelligence*

Emotional intelligence is the ability to understand, manage and communicate your emotions.

How do you feel that you handle your emotions, such as anger, grief, sadness or joy? You may be a very intelligent person with a high IQ, but you may feel out of control when a strong emotion suddenly arises, and find it difficult to integrate your emotions with your reasoning. Sudden anger or fear may seem to 'hijack' your mind. The good news is that with awareness and practice you can improve your emotional coping mechanisms. If you have trouble with your emotions, get help or take a workshop to enhance your emotional skills.

Make peace with food

When we've lost a spiritual connection in our lives, we may eat and eat in an attempt to fill an inner void.

Lynn Ginsberg and Mary Taylor, authors of *What Are You Hungry For?*

If you want a more balanced and more spiritual life, it's important to make peace with food. If you have problems with over-eating, constant dieting and worries about your body, look for a spiritual solution.

You may be eating to stuff down emotions that you don't want to feel, or you may be feeling that your value as a person is tied up with how you look. Start paying attention to what you're feeling, both physically and emotionally, when you want to over-eat. Begin to keep a journal of what issues come up for you. With time, you may find that you want to make art rather than eat that chocolate sundae. Or you may discover that you need self-love rather than that bag of crisps.

Rescue yourself from yourself

We're our own dragons as well as our own heroes, and we have to rescue ourselves from ourselves.

Tom Robbins, author of *Another Roadside Attraction*

We all have our dragons. Perhaps you have problems with addiction, or your anger sometimes gets the better of you. Maybe your dragon just can't get off the couch when there's work to be done. Or perhaps your dragon spends too much money at the shops.

In order to keep your dragons in line, you have to call on your hero – that part of you that is brave and true, that knows a problem when it sees one. If your dragons are overwhelming your life, visualize yourself as a hero: a knight, or Joan of Arc. Or if Spiderman works for you, great! Ask yourself what you, as a hero, can do to save yourself from the dragons in your life.

Create your own sand mandala

Art for the Tibetans is well accepted as a precious window into an alternative reality, into the enlightened dimension.

Marylin M. Rhie and Robert A. F. Thurman, authors of *Wisdom and Compassion*

In Tibetan Buddhism, the word *mandala* means 'circle'. Sand mandalas are forms of ritual art depicting sacred mansions, or the homes of particular meditation deities. Tibetan monks use brightly coloured sand to create the highly complicated mandala.

Both the deity and the mandala itself are considered manifestations of the Buddha's enlightened mind. The mandala is created with an understanding of impermanence and non-attachment. After it has been completed, it is eventually swept up and deposited in a river. Explore making your own sand mandala as a prayer for your own healing.

Don't get discouraged

One of the things I learned the hard way was that it doesn't pay to get discouraged.

Lucille Ball, comedian (1910–89)

Life is not easy. Problems arise on a daily basis. Success in one area of your life may be met with defeat in another. You may have started your own business and failed miserably. Or you may have written your first novel, only to be met with a stack of rejection letters.

Whether you're an optimist or a pessimist doesn't change the fact that life is difficult. The antidote to the reality of life is to not entertain discouragement. No matter what happens, keep your optimism intact. Stay active and keep your faith in yourself.

Cast off outworn beliefs

When you find a burden in belief or apparel, cast it off.

Amelia Jenkins Bloomer, champion of women's rights (1818–94)

As you grow older, you may find that beliefs that you had in your younger years no longer apply. You may have inherited the belief that only men can be scientists or religious leaders, yet as you grow older you realize this is false. Or your family may have held prejudices against people of colour, but you grow up and decide that racism is abhorrent. Or you may no longer believe in the religious dogma you learned as a child.

If you're dedicated to a lifetime of learning and personal growth, your beliefs will change and evolve. Consciously release beliefs that no longer fit who you are.

Let people cut in front of you

That guy just cut right in front of me. But I'm not going to let it bother me. No. I'm on my way to work and I decided it doesn't matter who wants to cut in front of my lane today. I'm not going to let it bother me one bit.
Oprah Winfrey, talkshow host (b. 1954)

Road rage is an international phenomenon. Somehow, no matter how shy and retiring you may be as pedestrian, when you get behind the wheel of a car, your primitive limbic brain often takes hold.

When someone cuts in front of you, you feel outraged at their reckless behaviour. You resent the fact that they're trying to get ahead of you. You may feel your blood pressure rise and your pulse race. You think terrible thoughts about the person, and step on the accelerator to try to pass them.

The next time someone cuts in front of you, skip all of the above. Wish the driver well. Preserve your peace and equanimity at all costs.

Let your ideas evolve

I begin with an idea and then it becomes something else.
Pablo Picasso, artist (1881–1973)

An idea is a living, breathing, organic thing. It's influenced by its environment and context. It can grow in size and take on new branches, or it can completely morph into something else. When newly hatched, it's like a chick – wobbly and wet-feathered. It needs to dry off, mature and find its way in the world.

If you have an idea for a business, an invention, a book or a way to help the homeless in your community, don't set it in concrete. Meet up with other people, give it time to incubate and let it evolve organically.

Exercise your brain

The brain is like a muscle. When it is in use we feel very good.
Understanding is joyous.
Carl Sagan, astronomer and author (1934–96)

If you want to enjoy life more, use your mind. Challenge yourself to contemplate difficult ideas. Read. Have intelligent discussions. Write your thoughts in a journal. Write emails or letters to your friends about what you're thinking.

Try to solve the big questions of life, like 'Why do I exist?', 'How big is the universe?' or 'How can we stop global warming?' Meditate on subjects like impermanence, or how an object can be simultaneously both a particle and a wave. Feel the exhilaration when you make a leap in understanding. Give your brain a workout as you would give your muscles a workout at the gym.

Keep playing

We don't stop playing because we grow old, we grow old because we stop playing.

George Bernard Shaw, dramatist (1856–1950)

Play is not just for children, or even just for humans. Animals play in order to practise for the hunt, to socialize, to keep fit, to stay alert and to enjoy themselves. Watch crows: they will throw a twig and then swoop down and catch it. Children play to learn motor skills, to practise being adults and to experience joy. Adults need to play to be creative, to experience joy and continue to learn. Yet it's extremely easy to forget how to play.

How can you bring play back into your life? If you're feeling inhibited, start playing more with your own or other people's kids. Play with your pets. Be more playful with your partner. Try to bring the spirit of play into every day.

Help yourself

Self-help must precede help from others. Even for making certain of help from heaven, one has to help oneself.
Moraji Desai, Indian government official (1896–1995)

You may want someone to come in and fix your life. You may long to be rescued from your problems. You may ask for God to intervene to remove your pain, pay your bills or find you a new job. But if you don't help yourself first nothing will happen.

The energy for help and change has to start with you. You have to pick up the phone and call a therapist, join a 12-step programme or negotiate with the debt collectors. You have to make an effort on your own behalf. You must reach out to the universe, if you want the universe to respond to you.

Try cinematherapy

I don't believe in psychology. I believe in good movies.
Bobby Fischer, chess champion (b. 1943)

Many therapists prescribe movies to help their patients heal their psyches. If you're not in therapy, try using movies on your own to help you sort through your problems.

There are many ways to approach this. Sometimes you just need a good cry, or a good laugh. A classic 'tear-jerker' or a slapstick comedy can provide that emotional release. On a deeper level, if you're having problems with your relationship with your father, mother or partner, or you're having difficulty with self-confidence, you might choose a movie that explores those themes. Ask yourself what you like or don't like about the characters, and if there are any that you admire and would like to emulate. How did the characters grow and resolve their problems?

Forget your reputation

Reputation is an idle and most false imposition; oft got without merit, and lost without deserving.
William Shakespeare, dramatist and poet (1564–1616)

There's a BBC TV comedy, shown around the world, called *Keeping Up Appearances*. It pokes fun at the age-old human desire to appear to be more, or better, than you actually are, or to be regarded in high esteem by your neighbours, colleagues and friends.

Because of the human tendency to project positive or negative traits onto others, your reputation often rests on others' projection of their disowned qualities onto you. Shakespeare understood well the false nature of reputation, and the futility of worrying about it. It's best to live a good, authentic life, and not concern yourself with what others think – positively or negatively.

Fertilize your soul

Life ought to be a struggle of desire towards adventures whose nobility will fertilize the soul.

Rebecca West, author and journalist (1892–1983)

Are you growing as a person? Are you living your life as an adventure? Are you feeding your soul? The soul hungers for meaning and purpose. It wants passion, experience, depth and realization. It wants to understand the meaning of life, be free from delusions and negative emotions. It wants to love freely, be patient, generous, kind and brave. It wants to be compassionate. Your soul wants to understand the divine and its place in the universe. Your job is to help feed your soul and fulfil its desires.

Write down ten ways in which you can fertilize your soul. Maybe you need to schedule some travel, learn to meditate or write a love letter.

Try alternative grains

In Greek mythology, grain is associated with Demeter, the archetypal mother of the human soul and the fruitful forces of nature.

Joanne Saltzman, author of *Amazing Grains*

Wheat is a staple in the diet of many different nations around the world. If you eat too much wheat, however, it's possible to develop a low-level food allergy.

Consider not eating wheat products for a month. Experiment with other grains for balance, including spelt, rye, quinoa, amaranth, barley, buckwheat, millet, kamut, rice, wild rice or corn. Eating grains in their whole form provides more fibre and nutrients than if you eat them as noodles or other flour products. Pressure-cooking speeds up the process. Combine whole grains with beans for a complete protein.

Kill the snake of doubt

Kill the snake of doubt in your soul, crush the worms of fear in your heart, and mountains will move out of your way.

Kate Seredy, children's writer and illustrator (1899–1975)

Sometimes it takes courage to doubt – when you question long-held beliefs or a relationship that no longer works. But when doubt and fear become a habit, they can undermine your soul. It's important to know the difference. If doubt and fear seem to be a constant theme in your life, you have a problem.

If you've chosen a course of action, a spiritual path or a new creative project, give your best energy to deciding if it's the right thing to do. Process any fear or doubt. Then, once you've made your decision, leave your doubt and fear at the doorstep. Enter your new venture without holding back. Put your full energy into the direction you've chosen. If you continue to entertain doubt and fear, you'll deprive yourself of the opportunity to grow and develop.

Discover your genius

Thousands of geniuses live and die undiscovered – either by themselves or by others.

Mark Twain, author and river pilot (1835–1910)

Genius isn't measured just by IQ tests. Genius can manifest as any innate capability or talent. You may be discounting your innate genius as a cook, an interior decorator, a writer, an artist, a gardener, a seamstress, a carpenter, a researcher, a healer, a masseuse, a mediator, a preacher, a public speaker, a politician or a car mechanic.

What are you 'good at'? It may be something you don't do for a living, so it may not seem that important to you. Ask others as well, for their assessment of your talents and capabilities. Honour your genius in whatever form it takes, and develop it for your own and others' benefit.

Be like Daruma

Fall seven times, stand up eight.

Japanese proverb

Daruma is the Japanese name for Bodhidharma, the 6th-century Indian patriarch who brought Zen Buddhism to Japan. Daruma was said to have spent nine years seated in meditation, losing the use of his arms and legs.

Legless Daruma dolls are popular all over Japan. They are weighted in the bottom so that they can't be easily tipped over. This is because Daruma is a symbol of great perseverance: he teaches us to rise no matter how many times we fall. People buy 'eyeless' Daruma dolls outside temples, and paint in one eye at the beginning of a project; the other eye is painted in when they achieve their goal.

The next time life seems to be handing you one failure after the next, remember Daruma's determination: get up and resolve to achieve your goals.

Lift weights

A few hours a week of training will give you a firmer, healthier-looking body as well as increased strength, which will carry over into other activities.

Thomas D. Fahey and Gayle Hutchinson, authors of *Weight Training for Women*

Weightlifting is not just for male body builders – it's also a great health and fitness practice for women. If you're a man, you'll enjoy increased strength, fitness and greater sex appeal. If you're a woman, you too will enjoy a more attractive body, increased strength and self-confidence. Strength training will also make your muscles, tendons and ligaments stronger and less susceptible to injury. For older women, lifting weights is an important deterrent for heart disease and osteoporosis.

Start with a set of hand weights to use at home, and get a good book for instruction. If weightlifting suits you, join a gym and get professional training on how to use free weights and machines.

Create yourself

But if you have nothing at all to create, then perhaps you create yourself.
Carl Jung, psychologist (1875–1961)

You don't have to create a painting, write a book or compose a symphony in order to be creative. Perhaps real creativity lies in developing yourself spiritually. Your capacity for spiritual and psychological development is enormous, yet you may neglect it for day-to-day material concerns.

Consider your life to be your creative expression. What can you do to enhance your understanding of yourself, your psychology and your spirituality? Commit to deepening your development through study, therapy and spiritual practice. Consider becoming enlightened for the benefit of all beings.

Deal with your insomnia

The best cure for insomnia is to get a lot of sleep.
W. C. Fields, actor and comedian (1880–1946)

If you have trouble sleeping, try the following remedies. Cut down on stimulants like tea, coffee and soft drinks. Reduce your sugar intake. Take a hot bath containing some lavender essential oil before bed. Go to sleep at the same time every night. Do a few yoga postures before going to bed. Don't eat anything after your evening meal. Listen to a CD of soothing music or nature sounds, such as ocean waves. Move the TV out of your bedroom. Try herbal remedies such as skullcap or valerian.

Write down what's worrying you before you go to sleep, and mentally let it go until morning. Sleep in a cool, dark, quiet room.

Live the truth

Truth isn't always beauty, but the hunger for it is.
Nadine Gordimer, novelist (b. 1923)

Sometimes the truth is hard to take. It may challenge you to do things or to make changes that you find frightening. Because of this, you may not want to face it. Therefore you choose to settle for less than you need or want, deny your responsibility in certain situations, and rationalize your behaviour to protect yourself.

For example, your relationship may be over, but you stay because it's too frightening to be on your own. Or you've hit a parked car – no one saw you, so you drive off. If you make the commitment to live the truth, you'll find the strength to face its demands. You will create an authentic, beautiful life.

Learn self-defence

In order to defend yourself against violence you must possess the ability to do so. This ability can only be achieved through training.
Mike Lorden, author of *Practical Self-Defence*

Whether you're a man or woman, it doesn't hurt to learn basic self-defence skills. Self-defence is usually taught separately from martial arts. Courses teach techniques to counter an actual physical attack, as well as greater awareness and crime prevention.

For women, special courses are available that utilize a padded attacker – a trained male wearing heavy protection from head to toe. This training affords you the opportunity to strike with full force, and learn what is effective in stopping an attack. If you have been the victim of an attack in the past, this training could prove invaluable for healing old wounds.

Do no harm

Half the harm in this world is due to the people who want to
feel important.

T. S. Eliot, poet (1888–1965)

One important guiding principle for life is 'Do no harm'. It sounds simple,
but it takes work and vigilance to actually live this maxim.

Like most people, you probably think first of yourself in any situation.
Your benefit, well-being and comfort are a guiding force in all your
actions. But what if you assessed all your actions according to whether
they would cause you or anyone else harm?

Try living for 24 hours without causing yourself – or anyone else –
harm. Does your life change in any way? Do you eat differently, speak to
others differently? Do you make different decisions about what you
purchase, or refrain from substance abuse? Are you a better parent or
partner, or more ethical in your actions?

Serve others through your work

Service is love in action, love 'made flesh'; service is the body, the incarnation of love.

Sarah Patton Boyle, activist and author of *The Desegregated Heart*

You need to earn a living, but the highest motivation for work is to serve others. If you manufacture or sell a product, make sure it helps people to live better lives. If you provide a service – be it counselling, plumbing, writing, tree-trimming, car repair, computer programming, healing or dog-grooming – give the best service you can, maintaining your client's happiness as your highest priority.

If you work for a company, make sure that you're comfortable with its business practices, its ethical standards and its relationship with its customers. Do the best you can to serve the company, your immediate boss and your colleagues, as well as your company's clients.

Shifting your motivation for work from money to service makes for a more uplifting, satisfying and rewarding life.

Sources

All sources are acknowledged below or directly under the relevant quotations. Every reasonable effort has been made to acknowledge the ownership of copyright material included in this book. Any errors that have inadvertently occurred will be corrected in subsequent editions provided notification is sent to the publisher.

Bartlett, Kaplan and Justin, John, *Bartlett's Familiar Quotations*, Little, Brown & Company, 2002

Bear, Sun, *Dancing With the Wheel*, Fireside, 1991

Blake, William, *The Complete Poetry and Prose of William Blake*, Anchor,

Bly, Robert, *A Little Book on the Human Shadow*, HarperSanFrancisco, 1988

Carson, Rachel, *The Sense of Wonder*, HarperCollins, 1987

Castaneda, Carlos, *The Teachings of Don Juan: A Yaqui Way of Knowledge*, Washington Square Press, 1985

Chödrön, Pema, *Awakening Loving Kindness*, Shambhala, 1996

Chödrön, Pema, *The Places That Scare You: A Guide to Fearlessness in Difficult Times*, Shambhala, 2001

The Columbia World of Quotations, Columbia University Press, 1998

Cousins, Norman, *Head First: The Biology of Hope and the Healing Power of the Human Spirit*, Penguin USA, 1990

De Balzac, Honoré, *The Magic Skin*, Indypublish.com, 2003

Delacroix, Eugène (Wellington, Herbert, trans.), *The Journal of Eugène Delacroix*, Phaidon Press, 1995

Dickinson, Emily, *The Collected Works of Emily Dickinson*, Reprint Services Corporation, 1999

Dunn-Mascetti, Manuela, *The Prayer Bead Box*, Viking Press, 2001

Easwaran, Eknath, *Love Never Faileth: Eknath Easwaran on St Francis, St Augustine, Mother Teresa and St Paul*, Nilgiri Press, 1996

Einstein, Albert, *Living Philosophies*, AMS Press, 1931

Fox, Matthew, *Creativity: Where the Divine and the Human Meet*, Tarcher/Putnam, 2002

Frank, Anne, *The Diary of a Young Girl: The Definitive Edition*, Bantam, 1997

Gibran, Kahlil, *The Prophet*, Knopf, 1966

Goettmann, Rachel, *Spiritual Wisdom and Practices of Early Christianity*, Inner Life Publications, 1994

Harrison, John, *Gardening for the Future of the Earth*, Bantam, 2000

Hubbard, Kin, *The Best of Kin Hubbard*, Indiana University Press, 1984

Le Guin, Ursula K., *Dancing at the Edge of the World: Thoughts on Words, Women, Places*, Grove Press, 1997

MacDougall, Alice Foote, *Autobiography of a Business Woman*, Ayer Company Publishing, 1980

Pagels, Elaine, *Beyond Belief: The Secret Gospel of St Thomas*, Random House, 2003

Quiller-Couch, Sir Arthur Thomas, *The Oxford Book of English Verse*, Oxford Clarendon, 1919

Rimpoche, Gehlek, unpublished transcript, Jewel Heart, Ann Arbor, MI

Rogers, Fred, *Mister Rogers Talks with Parents*, Berkeley Publishing Group, 1985

Rogers, Rutherford D., 'Torrent of Print Strains the Fabric of Libraries', *New York Times*, 25 March 1985

Schwartz, Barry, 'Economic Imperialism, the Market and Democracy', *The Battle for Human Nature: Science, Morality and Modern Life*, Norton, 1986

Selye, Hans, *Selye's Guide to Stress Research*, Van Nostrand Reinhold, 1980

Smith, Liz, gossip column, *New York Daily News*, 13 April 1986

Teresa, Mother, *The Joy in Loving: A Guide to Daily Living with Mother Teresa*, Penguin USA, 2000

Thoreau, Henry David, *Walden*, Houghton Mifflin, 1995

Twain, Mark, *What Is Man?*, Indypublish.com, 2003

Viorst, Judith, *Necessary Losses: The Loves, Illusions, Dependencies and Other Impossible Expectations that All of Us Have to Give Up in Order to Grow*, Free Press, 1998

Walljasper, Jay and Spayde, Jon, *Utne Reader*, *Visionaries: People and Ideas to Change Your Life*, New Society Publishers, 2001

Weil, Simone, *The Need for Roots: Prelude to a Declaration of Duties Towards Mankind*, Routledge, 2001

Whitman, Walt, *Leaves of Grass*, Bantam, 1983

Wilde, Oscar, *Two Plays by Oscar Wilde: An Ideal Husband and A Woman of No Importance*, Signet, 1997

Yutang, Lin, *The Importance of Living*, William Morrow, 1998

Index

acceptance 14, 90, 109
accidents 250
actions 128, 134, 135,
    190, 326
adventure 180
affirmations 343
age 83
air couriers, freelance 122
altars 319
anger 218
animals, rescue 95
appearances 196
appointments 301
appreciation 41, 153
artistic life 222
asking, needs 311
attention 121
authentic self see true
    natures
awareness 51

bartering 183
baths, Japanese 15
beans 17
beginner's mind 155
beliefs 357
bird-watching 165
body, accepting 109
brain see mind
bread 272
break-ups 336
breaks (rests) 120
breathing 35, 81
budgets 58
business, motivation 217

caffeine 220
carbohydrates 264
ceremonies 124
chakras 263
challenges 289
change 90, 150, 164
chanting 173
character 290
cheerfulness 334
children 110, 171, 313
choices 130, 294, 327
Christmas 194
cinema 363
cities 144
cleaning products 102
clothes 37, 49
clutter 13, 74, 252, 322
coin jars 269
commitments 299
communication 167
communities 117
compassion 105, 143
completeness, affirming
    174
compost 178
compromise 210
congruence 91
conscience 265
consumers 20
contentment 318
cooking 65, 278, 339
creativity 20, 222, 371
crying 186
crystals 349
curiosity 137
cycling 92

dancing 162, 309
Daruma 369
death 19, 213
debt 147, 198
decisions 140, 166
defeat 315
delight 157
democracy 177
demons (personal) 103
desires 330
destructive aspects 103
diet 50
    see also food
difficulties 108, 163
disagreements 175
disappointment 38
discontentment 273
discouragement 356
divine feminine 333, 342
doubt 367
dragons (personal) 354
dreams (aspirations) 168,
    216, 287
dreams (sleep) 22
dressing 37
drumming 284

ears 106
Earth, prayers for 61
eating in 65
ecological footprints 203
emotional intelligence
    352
energy 39, 292
energy bills 100
enjoyment 142

enthusiasm 119
equanimity 321
exercise 78
    cycling 92
    dancing 162, 309
    spine 286
    tai chi 344
    walking 60, 111
    weightlifting 370
    yoga 243, 286
expenses, small 350
experience 231
exuberance 159

failure 227
faith 257
family dinners 197
farmers' markets 275
fashion (clothes) 37, 49
fear 187
feminine, divine 333, 342
festivals 31
    Christmas 194
    New Year's Eve 73
    solstice 317
finance
    budgets 58
    children, teaching 171
    coin jar 269
    debt 147, 198
    income and expense
        charts 72
    jobs 63
    live within means 147
    past 21
    positive use 331
    records 66
    small expenses 350
    two-incomes 266
    worry about 191

finishing projects 244
flexibility 129
flowers 151
food
    beans 17
    caffeine 220
    carbohydrates 264
    frugal 69
    grains 366
    leftovers 267
    make peace with 353
    sacred 339
    soups 26
    sugar 18
    vegetables 253
    see also diet
forgiveness 138
friendships 30
frugal food 69
frugal living 68
future, creating 133

gardening 33, 158
genius 368
giving 40, 228, 311, 351
God 131, 324
good life 204
grace, saying 53
grains 366
grass 99
gratitude 25, 48
Green movement 192
greeting the soul 89
grief 246
guilt 32

habits 226, 281
happiness 214, 302
harm, doing no 375
healing 67, 156

heart, revolution of 296
herbal remedies 247
holidays, volunteer 113
home, feeling at 29, 136
honesty 70
hostels 79
houses 201
humour 276
    see also laughter
hurrying 200, 335

I Ching 341
ideals 231
ideas 359
images, violent 98
impermanence 57
impulse-buying 283
income and expense
    charts 72
information, managing 24,
    179
insomnia 372
inspiration 59
interdependence 47
Internet 39
intuition 338
investments 160

Japanese baths 15
jobs 63, 132, 184
journals 43, 258
joy 51, 159
judgement 14

karma 327
kindness 23, 316
kitchens 74
kites 303
knitting 240
knowledge 182

laughter 96, 118
  see also humour
lawns 116
leaders 230
leaps, taking 307
learning 83, 112
leaving things undone 12
leftover food 267
letters, love 36
librarians 291
life
  frugal 68
  good 204
  making the most of
    189, 294
  organizing 259
  responding to 323
  sweet 300
  yes to 310
life coaches 86
listening 44, 161
lists, to do 12, 19
love 193, 314
  letters 36
  people 332
  renewing 181
  work 132
love addiction 340
loving kindness 76
lunches 46
lying 254

mandalas, sand 355
massage 245
meditation
  breath 35
  completeness 174
  loving kindness 76
  sitting 237

mentoring 56
mind
  beginner's 155
  maintaining 112, 360
  open 304
  power of 85, 224
  purifying 229
  speaking your 207
mistakes 223
money see finance
moon 205
motivation 101, 217
music 84
mysterious 127
myths 346

nappies 176
naps 225
nature 60, 188, 280
necessities 28
needs 311, 316
new, trying something
  347
New Year's Eve 73

obesity 50, 264
open doors 38
open mind 304
optimism 154, 345
  see also positive thinking
organic gardening 158
origami 348

parents 260
passion, true 277
patience 42
peace, prayers for 64
people-pleasing 211
perfectionism 238

perseverance 369
pilgrimages 337
playing 361
pleasures, simple 302
positive energy 39
positive thinking 93
  see also optimism
possessions
  dematerialize 125
  letting go 212
  maintaining 241
  steward of 149
  as symbols 195
  worry about 191
power 206, 295
prayer beads 306
prayer flags 255
prayers
  centring 54
  Earth 61
  healing 67
  peace 64
  serenity 87
prejudice 146
present moment 145,
  221
priorities 215
projects
  finishing 244
  starting 239
purification 229

Quakers 308
questions 279

reading 293
reading groups 126
readjusting 297
records, financial 66

recovery, belief in 152
recycling 169
rejoicing 55
relationships 175, 336
relaxation 305
renting things 27
reputation 364
rest 34, 120, 225, 270
retreats 261
revenge 199
road rage 358
roots 136

sacred contract 268
sacred food 339
sacred sexuality 285
sacred sound 312
sand mandalas 355
schedules 208
seasons 317
secondhand items 271
self-acupressure 106
self-defence 374
self-help 362
self-respect 139
serenity prayer 87
service 282, 376
seven generations 166
sexuality 285
shadow 248
sharing 182, 183, 329
shopping
    consumers 20
    dematerialize 125
    farmers' markets 275
    food 69, 275
    impulse 283
    mail-order 273
    secondhand items 271

small expenses 350
    spaving 114
silence 80, 308
simple pleasures 302
simplicity 45, 274
singing 170
sitting meditation 237
skies 148
sleep 104, 270
smoking 249
solstice 317
soul 89, 202, 365
sound 312
soups 26
space-clearing 322
spaving 114
speaking your mind 207
speech, mindful 242
speed 335
spine 286
spiritual life 59, 236, 257
stars 16
starting projects 239
stress, counteracting 62
success 71
sugar 18
sunlight 75

tai chi 344
talents 295, 368
Tara 342
teaching 185
technology 219
television 82
thrift 68
tightwads 68
time 52
to do lists 12, 19

tragedies, response to 157
travel 79
trees, planting 97
true natures 123, 172, 251
trust 256
truth 328, 373
TV 82

uncertainty 262
uniqueness 141

vegetables 253
violent images 98
visionaries 107
voluntary work 94
volunteer holidays 113
voting 298

walking 60, 111
water 77
wealth, non-financial 25, 288
Web (World Wide) 39
weddings 88
weekends 305
weightlifting 370
whining 320
women's circle 325
work see jobs
work, voluntary 94
world, improving 209
World Wide Web 39
worrying 115, 191
wounds, healing 156
writing 36, 43, 258

yoga 243, 286

Acknowledgements

Cassini Textures by Crown Wallcoverings (Stockists tel: 0800 438 1554)
376; **Corbis UK Ltd**/Clayton J. Price 127; **Fired Earth Interiors**
www.firedearth.com (Stockists tel: +44 (0)1295 814300) 270; **Getty Images**
100, 138, 162, 164, 346, 363, 369/Roy Botterell 107/Dennie Cody 203/Roy
Corral 261/Jim Cummins 330/Davies & Starr 116/Jody Dole 83/Nick Dolding
303/Richard Kolker 147/Gerben Oppermans 141/Photodisc 24–25, 37, 49, 49,
71, 78, 79, 92, 95, 111, 122, 126, 155, 169, 185, 196, 198, 200, 219, 259,
283, 293, 319, 358, 361, 367, 370/Antonio M. Rosario 39/Miguel Salmeron
161/Keren Su 255/Julie Toy 171/David Vance 286/Angela Wyant 269;
Madonna Gauding 118, 131; **Nasa**/F.Hasler, M.Jentoft-Nilsen, H.Pierce,
K.Palaniappan and M.Manyin 235; **Octopus Publishing Group Limited** 1,
2–3, 4, 5, 6, 8, 9, 10–11, 12, 15, 17, 18, 20, 22, 26, 28, 30, 33, 34, 36, 41,
42, 45, 46, 47, 52, 54, 55, 57, 59, 60, 62, 65, 67, 69, 73, 74, 75, 77, 80,
84, 87, 88, 89, 90, 97, 98, 103, 104, 106, 108, 109, 113, 115, 121, 124,
129, 133, 134, 136, 137, 142, 145, 148, 149, 151, 153, 154, 156, 158,
159, 165, 166, 172, 174, 177, 179, 180, 181, 182, 183, 186, 188, 190,
192, 194, 201, 205, 206, 208, 211, 213, 214, 215, 216, 220, 222, 225 left,
225 right, 227, 229, 232-233, 234, 236, 237, 238, 240, 243, 244, 247,
248, 251, 253, 257, 258, 263, 264, 267, 272, 275, 276, 279, 280, 284,
285, 289, 291, 294, 296, 299, 301, 302, 305, 306, 308, 310, 312, 314,
317, 321, 323, 324, 327, 329, 333, 335, 337, 338, 339, 341, 345, 348,
349, 351, 353, 357, 366, 372, 375; **Rubberball Productions** 328, 365;
Luzia Strohmayer 209, 231; **TopFoto**/Kent Meireis/The Image Works 355

Executive Editor Brenda Rosen
Managing Editor Clare Churly
Executive Art Editor Sally Bond
Designer Pia Hietarinta for Cobalt id
Production Controller Aileen O'Reilly